Macmillan Computer Science Series

A. Abdellatif, J. Le Bihan, M. Limame, *Oracle - A User's*
Ian O. Angell, *High-resolution Computer Graphics Using*
Ian O. Angell and Gareth Griffith, *High-resolution Comp*
C. Bamford and P. Curran, *Data Structures, Files and Databases, second edition*
P. Beynon-Davies, *Database Systems*
P. Beynon-Davies, *Information Systems Development, third edition*
Linda E.M. Brackenbury, *Design of VLSI Systems – A Practical Introduction*
Alan Bradley, *Peripherals for Computer Systems*
P.C. Capon and P.J. Jinks, *Compiler Engineering Using Pascal*
B.S. Chalk, *Computer Organisation and Architecture*
Eric Davalo and Patrick Naïm, *Neural Networks*
Joyce Duncan, Lesley Rackley and Alexandria Walker, *SSADM in Practice
 – A Version 4 Text*
D. England *et al.*, *A Sun User's Guide, second edition*
Jean Ettinger, *Programming in C++*
J.S. Florentin, *Microprogrammed Systems Design*
Michel Gauthier, *Ada - A Professional Course*
M.G. Hartley, M. Healey and P.G. Depledge, *Mini and Microcomputer Systems*
M.J. King and J.P. Pardoe, *Program Design Using JSP – A Practical Introduction,
 second edition*
Bernard Leguy, *Ada - A Programmer's Introduction*
M. Léonard, *Database Design Theory*
David Lightfoot, *Formal Specification Using Z*
A.M. Lister and R.D. Eager, *Fundamentals of Operating Systems, sixth edition*
Tom Manns and Michael Coleman, *Software Quality Assurance, second edition*
G.P. McKeown and V.J. Rayward-Smith, *Mathematical Foundations for Computing*
B.A.E. Meekings, T.P. Kudrycki and M.D. Soren, *A book on C, third edition*
R.J. Mitchell, *C++ Object-oriented Programming*
R.J. Mitchell, *Microcomputer Systems Using the STE Bus*
R.J. Mitchell, *Modula-2 Applied*
J.P. Pardoe and M.J. King, *Object Oriented Programming Using C++*
Pham Thu Quang and C. Chartier-Kastler, *MERISE in Practice*
Ian Pratt, *Artificial Intelligence*
F.D. Rolland, *Programming with VDM*
Z.M. Sikora, *Oracle Database Principles*
S. Skidmore, *Introducting Systems Analysis, second edition*
S. Skidmore, *Introducing Systems Design, second edition*
A.G. Sutcliffe, *Human-Computer Interface Design, second edition*
C.J. Theaker and G.R. Brookes, *Concepts of Operating Systems*
M. Thorin, *Real-time Transaction Processing*
D.J. Tudor and I.J. Tudor, *Systems Analysis and Design – A Comparison of
 Structured Methods*
A.J. Tyrrell, *Eiffel Object-Oriented Programming*

Computer Organisation and Architecture

An Introduction

B.S. Chalk

School of Computing Information Systems and Mathematics
South Bank University, London

MACMILLAN

First published 1996 by
MACMILLAN PRESS LTD
Houndmills, Basingstoke, Hampshire RG21 6XS
and London
Companies and representatives
throughout the world

ISBN 0–333–64551–0

A catalogue record for this book is available
from the British Library.

10   9   8   7   6   5   4   3
05   04   03   02   01   00   99   98

Printed in Great Britain by
Antony Rowe Ltd, Chippenham, Wiltshire

Contents

Preface

A computer is a versatile machine, capable of performing a wide range of tasks. At the heart of the machine lies a primitive language processor, which is interconnected with other functional units to provide a hardware platform for running programs. Computer organisation is a term used to describe the operation and interconnection of these functional units while computer architecture describes how the hardware platform appears to a machine language programmer.

The aim of this book is to provide a sufficiently detailed coverage of computer organisation and architecture to meet the needs of students on first year degree and HND courses in Computer Studies, Information Technology, Software Engineering and related areas of study. The material is also suitable for students taking conversion courses in areas such as Advanced Information Technology, Computer Science or for anyone wishing to gain a basic understanding of how a computer works. Apart from a rudimentary understanding of high-level language programming, no other prior level of knowledge is assumed.

The book adopts an interactive approach and supports self-study, by including an extensive number of Text Questions (TQs) for self-assessment purposes. Answers to TQs are given at the end of each chapter, together with a set of further exercises. Selected answers to these exercises are given at the back of the book.

Because of its widespread use as a teaching tool, I have adopted the Motorola 68000 as a vehicle for explaining the principles of processor operation and assembly language programming. Readers familiar with Intel or other processors should have no difficulty in adapting the concepts and program examples to other machines.

The book is divided into ten chapters. Chapters 1 to 7 include the basic core material we use at South Bank University for teaching one semester units in Computer Systems Architecture, Computer and Communication Architecture and Computer Systems Technology. Chapter 8, which provides an introduction to operating systems, is included to bridge the gap between Computer Architecture and System Software – a unit normally undertaken shortly afterwards. Chapters 9 and 10 introduce the more advanced topics of RISC and Parallel architectures. These topics have been included to illustrate the current trend in architectural development and to provide a foundation for second level units in subjects such as Microprocessor Technology and Concurrent Systems.

B.S. Chalk

Acknowledgements

I would like to begin by thanking Dr Mike Oatey for the many suggestions he made during the planning stage of this book. I would also like to thank: Terry Roberts, Ian Marshall and other students for giving me useful feedback on the text questions; Graham Davies, Bob Hine, Pirooz Saeedi and John Hill for their assistance in developing this material over the years; Audrey Curnock for her advice on presentation; Professor Frank Sumner for his comments and suggestions; and Malcolm Stewart from Macmillan Press, for steering the book through its various stages. Last but not least, I would like to thank my wife Anne for her encouragement and support.

London, March 1996

1 Introduction

Although electronic computers vary in size, cost and performance, the vast majority of general purpose computers are based on a model proposed by John von Neumann and others in 1946. In this chapter we will describe this model and relate its logical units to the physical components found in a typical micro-computer. This will provide a foundation for a more detailed discussion of computer organisation in subsequent chapters.

1.1 The von Neumann Computer Model

A key feature of this model is the concept of a *stored program*. A *program* is a set of *instructions* that describe the steps involved when carrying out a computational task, such as accessing a database or wordprocessing a document. The program is stored in memory together with any *data* upon which the instructions operate, as illustrated in figure 1.1.

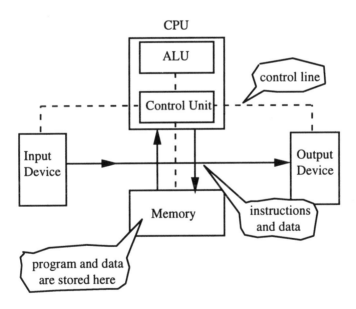

Figure 1.1 Structure of a von Neumann computer

To run a program, the CPU or *Central Processing Unit* repeatedly fetches, interprets and executes the instructions one after the other in a sequential manner.

This is carried out by a part of the CPU called the *control unit*. The execution phase frequently involves fetching data, altering it in some way and then writing it

1

back to memory. For this to be possible, an instruction must specify both the *operation* to be performed and the location or *memory address* of any data involved. Operations such as addition and subtraction are performed by a part of the CPU called the *Arithmetic and Logic Unit* (ALU).

Input and Output devices are needed to transfer information to and from memory. To sequence these transfers and to enforce the orderly movement of instructions and data in the system, the control unit uses various control lines.

1.2 A Microcomputer System

Figure 1.2 shows some of the basic *hardware* of a 'stand alone' microcomputer system. The system unit houses the bulk of the electronics, including the CPU and memory. Attached to this are various *peripheral devices*, such as a keyboard, a mouse, a Cathode Ray Tube (CRT) display and a printer. These devices provide the Input/Output (IO) facility.

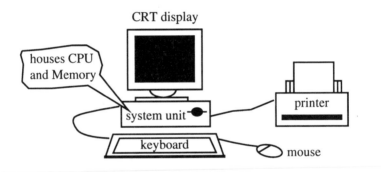

Figure 1.2 Basic microcomputer system

If we open the system unit and take a look inside, we find a number of electronic components mounted on a large *printed circuit* board, as shown in figure 1.3. The components are connected together by conducting *tracks*, for carrying electrical signals between them. These signals carry information in quantised or digital form and are therefore referred to as *digital signals*.

Most of the electronic components are in the form of *integrated circuits* (ICs), which are circuits built from small slices or 'chips' of the semiconductor material, *silicon*. The chips are mounted in plastic or ceramic packages to provide pins for connecting them to the printed circuit board. One of the largest and most complex ICs on the board is the *microprocessor*, which is the CPU of the system. This chip contains millions of electronic switches called *transistors* organised in the form of *logic gates*, the basic building blocks of digital circuits. These logic gates are used to implement the control unit, the ALU and other components of the CPU such as its *register set*. Logic gates are discussed in chapter 2.

There are two basic types of semiconductor memory on the printed circuit board, *Random Access Memory* (RAM) which is a read-write memory and *Read*

Only Memory (ROM). These form the fast *primary* or *main memory* of the system and both store information in *binary form* (1's and 0's). RAM is often provided in the form of *memory modules,* each module containing eight or nine memory chips. These modules are plugged into slots on the printed circuit board.

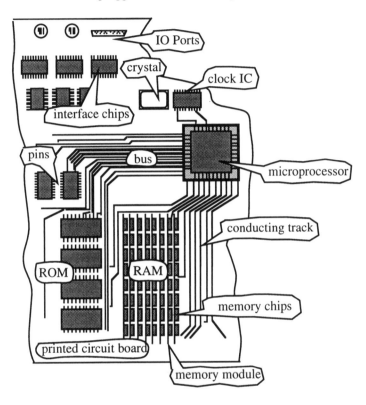

Figure 1.3 Showing part of the printed circuit board

Because RAM can be read from and written to, it is suitable for storing programs and data. Unfortunately RAM chips are normally *volatile* and therefore lose their content when the computer's power is switched off. ROM's on the other hand are *non-volatile* and are used for storing various *system programs* and data that needs to be available when the computer is switched on.

TQ 1.1   Why is ROM unsuitable for storing user programs?

In addition to a fast main memory, the microcomputer also has a large but slower *secondary* memory, usually in the form of a *hard disk* and one or two *floppy disk* units. Programs are stored on disk as *files* and must be loaded into main memory before they can be executed by the processor. Computer memory is discussed in chapter 6.

   The microprocessor or *processor* for short, is connected to memory and the other parts of the system by a group of conducting tracks called a *system bus*, which provides a pathway for the exchange of data and control information. Logically a system bus is divided into an *address bus*, a *data bus* and a *control bus*. To coordinate activities taking place inside the processor with those taking place on the system bus, some form of timing is required. This is provided by a crystal controlled *clock* IC.

   The Input/Output (IO) ports, shown at the top of figure 1.3, are used for connecting peripheral devices to the system. In general, peripheral devices operate at much slower speeds than the CPU and require special interface chips for connecting them to the system bus. Interfacing is discussed in chapter 7.

1.3 Representing Memory

We can visualise main memory as a series of storage boxes or locations, as shown in figure 1.4. Each location is identified by an *address* and can be used to store an instruction or some data. For example, the instruction *move 4*, is stored at address 0 and the datum, 2, is stored at address 5.

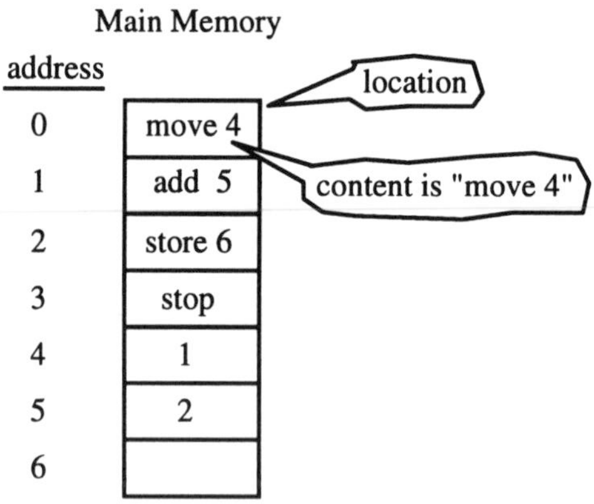

Main Memory

address	
0	move 4
1	add 5
2	store 6
3	stop
4	1
5	2
6	

location

content is "move 4"

Figure 1.4 A representation of memory

   The first instruction, *move 4*, moves the 'contents of address 4' or number *1*, in to one of the processor's registers. The second instruction, *add 5*, adds the 'contents of address 5' or number 2, to the first number stored in the register. The third instruction, *store 6*, stores the 'contents of this register' or the sum of the two numbers, into address 6. Finally the last instruction, *stop*, halts or prevents any further execution of the program.

1.4 High and Low-Level Languages

Instructions such as *move* and *add* are called *machine instructions* and are the only instructions the processor can 'understand' and execute. Writing programs at this level requires a knowledge of the computer's *architecture*, which includes amongst other things, details of the processor's registers, the different instructions it can execute (*instruction set*) and the various ways these instructions can address memory (*addressing modes*). Programming at machine level is called *low-level language* programming.

When we wish to write programs to solve particular problems, it is often easier to write them in English-like statements using a *High-Level Language* (HLL), such as Pascal or C. For example, the HLL statement:

$$SUM := A + B$$

gives the same result as our previous program while being easier to follow. The fact that the *variables* A, B and SUM refer to memory addresses 4, 5 and 6 or some other locations is hidden from the programmer and allows him or her to concentrate on the logic of the problem rather than the organisation of the computer.

Because the machine cannot directly interpret HLL program statements, these statements must be translated in to *machine instructions* before the program can be executed. Translating a HLL into *machine language* is the responsibility of a piece of *system software* called a *compiler*.

1.5 The Operating System

As well as software for solving user problems (*application software*), software is also needed for carrying out various system tasks, such as controlling the CRT display, reading the keyboard, loading files into memory from the hard disk, and so on. These programs are part of a powerful piece of *system software* called the *operating system*.

When we switch on a microcomputer, we are presented with some form of *user interface*. The interface might be graphical, as shown in figure 1.5 (a), or command driven, as shown in figure 1.5(b). In either case, the operating system creates an environment for the user to conveniently examine files and run programs. For a *Graphical User Interface* (GUI), this is done by 'clicking' on icons using a pointing device such as a mouse, while for a *Command Driven Interface*, it is done by entering special commands and file names from the keyboard.

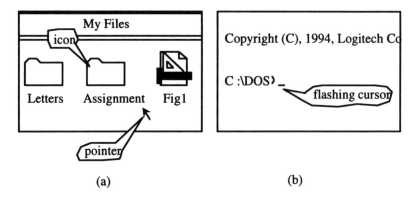

Figure 1.5 Different User Interfaces (a) Graphical (b) Command Driven

The fact that we do not have to know where a file is stored on disk or the main memory locations into which a program is loaded is simply due to the operating system.

Many operating system functions are either invisible to the user, or only become apparent when things go wrong, such as when an error occurs. We will return to the topic of operating systems in chapter 8.

1.6 Answers to Text Questions

TQ 1.1   Because they can only be read from and not written to, they cannot be loaded with user programs.

1.7 Exercises

1.   What do the letters CPU, RAM, ROM stand for?

2.   Write down the main features of a von Neumann style computer.

3.   Why do we need ROM in a microcomputer system?

4.   What do we mean by the terms *machine instruction* and *instruction set*?

5.   Which parts of the CPU are used for (a) fetching and interpreting instructions, (b) performing arithmetic operations such as 'add'?

6.   What are the advantages of programming in a high-level language?

7.   Software can be classified as either application software or system software. Give an example of each type.

8.   When porting software from one type of machine to another, it needs to be recompiled. Why is this?

9.   From the time you 'double-click' on an icon, such as a text document, to the time it appears on the screen and you are able to edit it, the operating system must perform a number of tasks. Outline what you think these might be.

2 Digital Logic Circuits

In chapter 1 we mentioned that logic gates were the basic building blocks of a digital computer. This chapter describes these gates and how they can be used to build useful circuits.

2.1 Logic Gates

Integrated circuits such as microprocessors, RAMs, interface chips and so on, are manufactured by putting hundreds or thousands of simple *logic gates* on to a silicon chip. The chip is then packaged to provide pins for connecting the circuit to the rest of the system, as illustrated in figure 2.1.

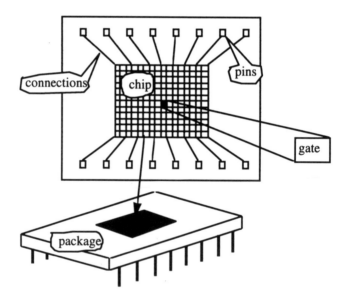

Figure 2.1 Relationship between chip, logic gate and package

Each logic gate generates an output that depends on the electronic logic level applied to its input(s). For two-state logic devices, the logic levels are described as either: true/false, high/low, on/off or 1/0.

Only a few basic types of gate are needed to build digital circuits, each gate performing a particular *logic function* such as AND, OR, or NOT. We represent these gates using special symbols, as shown in figure 2.2.

Name	Graphic symbol	Truth Table
AND	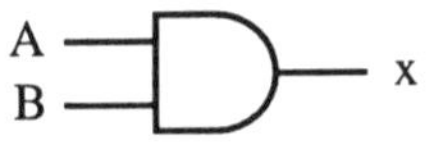	A B|x 0 0|0 0 1|0 1 0|0 1 1|1
OR		A B|x 0 0|0 0 1|1 1 0|1 1 1|1
NOT	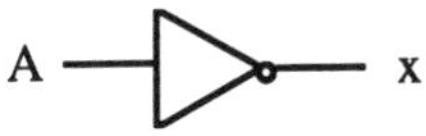	A|x 0|1 1|0
NAND	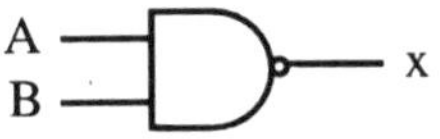	A B|x 0 0|1 0 1|1 1 0|1 1 1|0
NOR	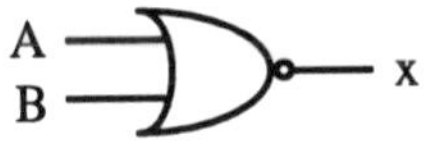	A B|x 0 0|1 0 1|0 1 0|0 1 1|0
Exclusive-OR		A B|x 0 0|0 0 1|1 1 0|1 1 1|0

Figure 2.2 Digital logic gates

.The input and output logic levels applied to these gates are represented by *boolean variables*, such as A, B and x. These variables can only take the values 1 or 0. For simplicity we have only considered dual-input gates, but it should be remembered that apart from the NOT gate, all other gates can have 2, 3, or more inputs, the upper limit depending upon the technology used to implement the gate.

The function of each logic gate is described by a *truth-table* which relates its input logic state to its output logic state. For example, the truth-table of the AND gate shows that the two inputs can take the values 00, 01, 10 or 11 and that the output value is only 1 when the input is 11.

TQ 2.1   What is the output value of an Exclusive-OR gate if just one of its inputs is at logic 1?

TQ 2.2   If the output value of a NAND gate is 0, then what can we deduce about its inputs?

TQ 2.3   Sometimes we describe a NOT gate as an inverter. Why?

2.2 Combinational Logic Circuits

By connecting simple logic gates together in various ways, we can build a whole range of useful circuits. In this section we will illustrate this with a few simple examples.

(1) Half-adder

Figure 2.3(a) is a circuit called a *half-adder*, which can be built using an AND gate in combination with an Exclusive-OR gate.

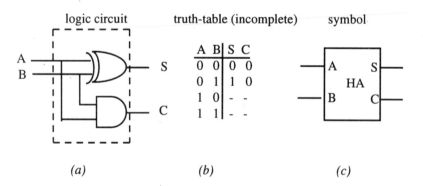

logic circuit	truth-table (incomplete)	symbol

A	B	S	C
0	0	0	0
0	1	1	0
1	0	-	-
1	1	-	-

(a)   (b)   (c)

Figure 2.3 Half-adder

    The circuit has two inputs, labelled A,B and two outputs, labelled S,C. From the AND and Exclusive-OR truth tables, we can see that when A and B are both at logic 0, that both S and C are also at logic 0. If we now take B to logic 1, then S also goes to logic 1, while C remains at logic 0.

TQ 2.4   Complete the truth-table in figure 2.3(b).

The half-adder, represented symbolically in figure 2.3(c), is used as a building block for a more useful circuit called a *full-adder*.

(2) Full-adder

A full-adder is shown in figure 2.4(a). It is a combinational logic circuit with three inputs, labelled A, B, C_i and two outputs, labelled S and C_o. The circuit is used to find the sum S of pairs of binary digits, A and B. C_o is 1 if a carry-out is generated and is 0 otherwise. C_i or carry-in, is used to allow any carry generated by adding other pairs of digits to be included in the sum. In (§3.5) we will describe how a chain of these full-adders can be used to add binary numbers together.

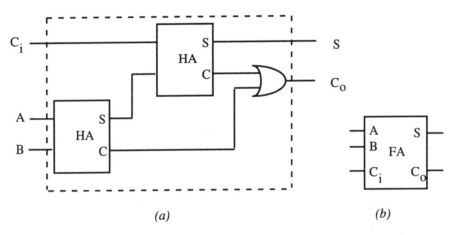

(a)   (b)

Figure 2.4 (a) Full-adder (b) Circuit symbol

The truth-table for this circuit is given in the following table.

Table 2.1 Truth-Table for a full-adder

A	B	C_i	S	C_o
0	0	0	0	0
0	1	0	1	0
1	0	0	1	0
1	1	0	0	1
0	0	1	1	0
0	1	1	0	1
1	0	1	0	1
1	1	1	1	1

(3) 2-to-4 decoder

Another useful circuit is the 2-to-4 line decoder shown in figure 2.5, which can be built from a combination of NAND and NOT gates. The NOT gates are arranged in such a way that each of the four input combinations 00, 01, 10, 11 activates a different NAND gate, by taking both of its inputs 'high'. This forces the output of the NAND gate to go 'low'. The inputs A,B are therefore used to select one and only one of the outputs $\overline{S0},...,\overline{S3}$, by forcing it to go low.

This circuit can be used for address decoding, which we discuss in (§6.4).

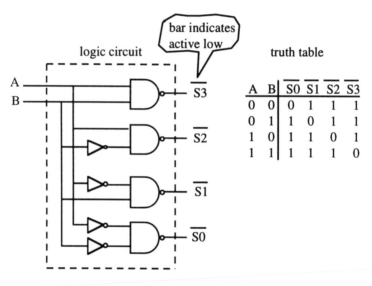

A	B	$\overline{S0}$	$\overline{S1}$	$\overline{S2}$	$\overline{S3}$
0	0	0	1	1	1
0	1	1	0	1	1
1	0	1	1	0	1
1	1	1	1	1	0

Figure 2.5 2-to-4 decoder

(4) 2-input multiplexer

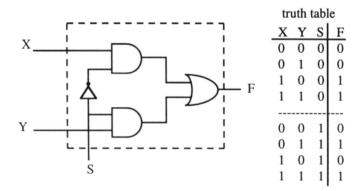

truth table

X	Y	S	F
0	0	0	0
0	1	0	0
1	0	0	1
1	1	0	1
0	0	1	0
0	1	1	1
1	0	1	0
1	1	1	1

Figure 2.6 2-input multiplexer

This circuit has three inputs X, Y, S and one output F. From the truth table you will notice that when S=0, the output F is the same as the input X, and when S=1, the output F is the same as the input Y. In other words, the circuit acts as a logic switch, the output F being connected to X or Y depending upon whether S=1 or S=0.

2.3 Sequential Logic Circuits

Combinational logic circuits, where the output depends solely on the current state of the input, are useful for implementing functional units such as adders or switches. However, for memory elements and other functional units that have outputs that depend upon their current input and the current state of the circuit we need to use sequential logic elements. The simplest form of sequential logic circuit is the *flip-flop*.

(1) R-S flip-flop

Figure 2.7 is a NOR gate version of an R-S flip-flop, the NOR gates being labelled G1 and G2. The circuit has two inputs, labelled R, S and two outputs, labelled Q and Q̄. The bar over the latter Q (pronounced 'not Q'), indicates that this output is the complement or inverse of Q.

The circuit can exists in one of two stable states by virtue of the fact that its outputs are cross-coupled to its inputs. For this reason we call this type of circuit a *bistable* device.

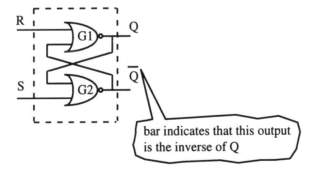

Figure 2.7 NOR gate version of an R-S flip-flop

With the inputs and outputs shown in figure 2.8(a), the circuit is in the first of its two stable states. We can check this by referring to the truth table of the NOR gate given in figure 2.2, and noting that the output of a NOR gate is always 0 if either or both of its inputs are at logic 1. Because the output Q from gate G1 is also an input to G2, then when Q = 0 and S = 0 the output Q̄ is 1. This output is fed-back to G1 and holds Q = 0, irrespective of whether R = 0 or R = 1.

When S is taken to logic 1, as shown in figure 2.8(b), $\overline{Q}$ goes low forcing the Q output of G1 to 1, since both its inputs are now low. The output of G1 is fed-back to G2 and holds $\overline{Q}$ low, so that when S is restored to 0, as shown in figure 2.8(c), the outputs remain in this second stable state.

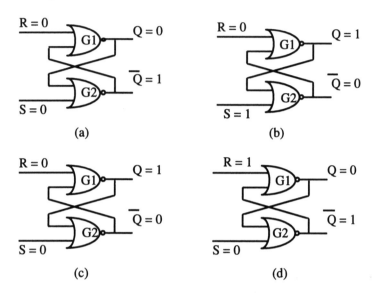

(a)   (b)

(c)   (d)

Figure 2.8 Operation of an R-S flip-flop circuit

TQ 2.5   Describe what happens if R is now taken high then low.

The R or *Reset* input is used to restore the circuit to its original state, while the input S is called Set, because it sets the circuit into a second stable state.

(2) Clocked R-S flip-flop

A clocked R-S flip-flop circuit is shown in figure 2.9.

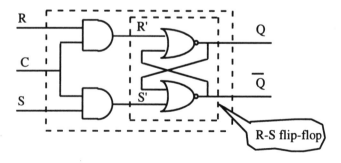

Figure 2.9 Clocked R-S flip-flop

In this circuit, inputs R and S are ANDed with a third *clock* input C. The outputs of the AND gates (R' and S') then act as inputs to the R-S flip-flop.

TQ 2.6   When $C = 0$, what will the values of R' and S' be?

Only when $C = 1$ do the R' and S' inputs take on the input values R and S and affect the output of the circuit. The circuit therefore acts as a clock controlled storage element. When the clock is high, a '1' can be stored at the Q output by taking $S = 1$ and $R = 0$ and a '0' can be stored by taking $R = 1$ and $S = 0$. When the clock goes low, the information (either '1' or '0') stored in the *memory element* is protected from alteration.

(3) D-type flip-flop

A simple D-type flip-flop circuit is shown in figure 2.10. It is basically a clocked R-S flip-flop with the R-input connected by a NOT gate to the S-input.

TQ 2.7   When $D = 1$ what will the values R and S be?

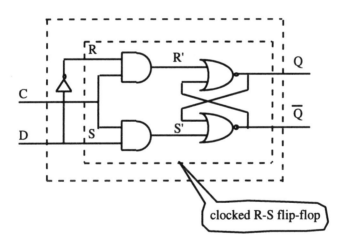

Figure 2.10 D-type flip-flop circuit

We can illustrate the way in which data is clocked or *latched* into this type of storage element, by using a timing diagram as shown in figure 2.11.

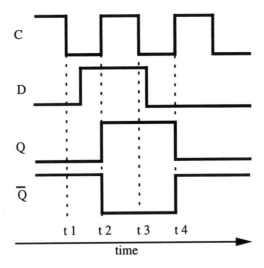

Figure 2.11 Timing diagram for the D-type flip-flop

The clock input C is a train of pulses which change from high-to-low at instants t1 and t3, and from low-to-high at instants t2 and t4. Only when C goes high is the flip-flop able to respond by changing its Q output to that of the D-input. For example, despite the fact that D goes high shortly after time t1, it is not until t2, when the clock also goes high, that output Q goes high. When C goes low again at instant t3, the output $Q = 1$, $\overline{Q} = 0$ is 'frozen' or *latched* by the flip-flop.

TQ 2.8   If the D input was to change during the period t2 to t3, then what would happen, if anything, to the output?

D-type flip-flops that latch data on the *transition* or edge of the clock rather than on its voltage level, are shown in figure 2.12. A transition can either occur on the rising or positive-edge of the clock when it goes from a low-to-high voltage, or on the negative-edge of the clock when it goes from a high-to-low voltage. Edge triggered D-type flip-flops can be used for building registers, shift registers and counters.

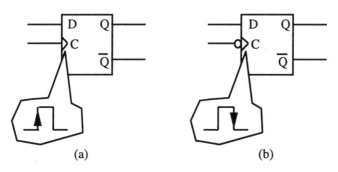

Figure 2.12 D-type flip-flops (a) Positive-edge triggered (b) Negative-edge triggered

2.4 D-type Flip-Flop Circuits

(1) Simple register

A parallel register is a group of memory elements that can be read or written to simultaneously. For the circuit shown in figure 2.13, the pattern of 1s and 0s supplied by the data inputs I0,..,I3 is stored by the D-type memory elements when the write data strobe line is activated.

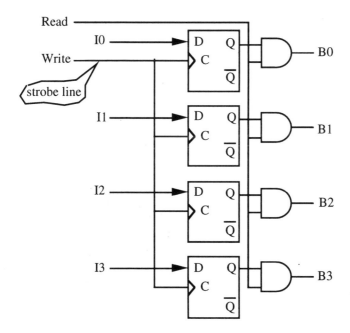

Figure 2.13 4-bit parallel register

Once stored, the data can be read in parallel from the B0,..,B3 output lines using the read control line.

TQ 2.9   What logic level would the read line have to be for the B0,..,B3 outputs
          to reflect the state of the Q outputs?

---

(2) Shift register

A shift register is a special type of register which accepts and/or transfers information serially. For the circuit shown in figure 2.14, the information in the form of 1's and 0's is applied to the leftmost flip-flop one digit or bit at a time.

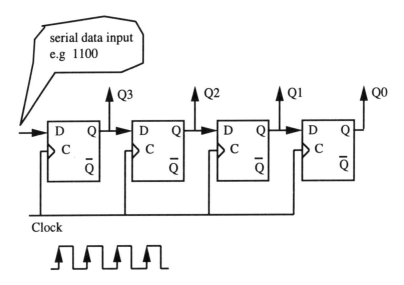

Figure 2.14 4-bit shift register

A *shift clock* applies clock pulses simultaneously to all the flip-flops, so that each time the circuit is clocked, the bit present at each D-input is transferred to its Q output. Therefore if the serial data arriving at the leftmost flip-flop happened to be 1100, then after four clock pulses it would have been shifted into the register and be stored as Q3 = 1, Q2 = 1, Q1 = 0 and Q0 = 0. Using a set of AND gates and a read line (not shown), this data could then be read from the register in parallel form, allowing the circuit to perform serial-to-parallel data conversion. Serial-Input-Parallel-Output (SIPO) shift registers are used in serial interface circuits, as described in §7.3.

(3) Binary up-counter

A counter is a circuit that passes through a sequence of well defined states on each transition of an input clock. Figure 2.15 is an example of an *asynchronous binary counter*, the outputs Q2, Q1, Q0 displaying the sequence 000, 001, 010, 011,... after each clock pulse. This is the way we count upwards in the *binary number system* (see §3.3).

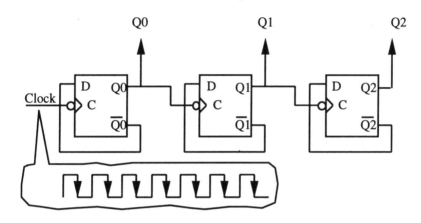

Figure 2.15 Asynchronous binary up-counter

The circuit uses three negative-edge triggered D-type flip-flops. The leftmost flip-flop or first stage of the counter is connected to the input clock, the other flip-flops being clocked from the output of their adjacent stages. The input to each flip-flop is derived from its $\overline{Q}$ output. The three outputs Q0, Q1 and Q2 are initially reset to zero.

TQ 2.10   What will the three $\overline{Q}$ outputs be initially?

The operation of this counter is best understood by referring to the timing diagram shown in figure 2.16.

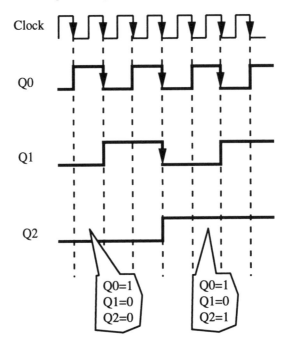

Figure 2.16 Timing diagram for the asynchronous counter

When the first clock transition takes place, the output Q0 changes from 0 to 1, because its D-input comes from its $\overline{Q0}$ output, which is 1. As Q0 changes to 1, $\overline{Q0}$ changes to 0, so that on the second clock transition, Q0 returns to 0 again. The Q0 output is therefore a train of clock pulses having half the frequency of the input clock. In a similar way, the Q1 output is a train of pulses having half the frequency of the Q0 output, which is therefore a quarter of the input clock frequency. The values of Q0, Q1 and Q2 after each transition are recorded in the table below.

Table 2.2 The output from the binary counter

clock transition	Q2	Q1	Q0
0	0	0	0
1	0	0	1
2	0	1	0
3	0	1	1
4	1	0	0
5	1	0	1
6	1	1	0
7	1	1	1

After reaching the state Q2 = 1, Q1 = 1, Q0 = 1, any further transitions of the clock will cause this sequence to be repeated.

This form of counter has the disadvantage of introducing delays between successive outputs owing to the signal rippling through the stages. For example, when counting from 011 → 100, the change in the output from the first stage is used to trigger the second stage which in turn triggers the third stage, before the final output becomes stable. For this reason, this type of counter is called an asynchronous or ripple-through counter. Counters which do not suffer from this problem are called synchronous counters.

2.5 Answers to Text Questions

TQ 2.1   The output will be at logic 1.

TQ 2.2   Both inputs must be at logic 1.

TQ 2.3   Because its output is always in the opposite logic state to its input.

TQ 2.4

A	B	S	C
0	0	0	0
0	1	1	0
1	0	1	0
1	1	0	1

TQ 2.5   If R is taken high, then Q goes low forcing $\bar{Q}$ high. $\bar{Q}$ holds G1 low so that the outputs remain unchanged when R returns to 0. The circuit is now in its original state.

TQ 2.6   Both $R' = 0$ and $S' = 0$

TQ 2.7 $R = 0$ and $S = 1$.

TQ 2.8   While the clock is high, the output will follow the D input.

TQ 2.9   The read line would need to be taken 'high', so that if the corresponding Q output was high, the AND gate would signal 1 and if the Q output was 'low', the AND gate would signal 0.

TQ 2.10   Each $\bar{Q}$ output will initially be 1.

2.6 Exercises

1. Complete the truth tables for the following circuit.

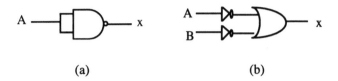

    (a)   (b)

    In each case suggest another gate that will perform the same logic function.

2. What is the difference between combinational logic and sequential logic?

3. Draw a diagram of an R-S flip-flop.

4. A clocked R-S flip-flop can be built from 4 NAND gates. Draw a diagram of a suitable circuit.

5. Draw a diagram of an 8-bit SIPO shift register.

6. If the D-type flip-flops in figure 2.15 were replaced by positive-edge triggered devices, then write down the new output sequence produced by the counter. Assume that the counter is initialised with $Q0 = Q1 = Q2 = 1$.

References

Mitchell, R.J. (1995), *Microprocessor Systems*, Macmillan Press Ltd, pp. 30-79.

3 Data Representation and Computer Arithmetic

Data is represented and stored in a computer using groups of binary digits called words. This chapter begins by describing binary codes and how words are used to represent characters. It then concentrates on the representation of positive and negative integers and how binary arithmetic is performed within the machine. The chapter concludes with a discussion on the representation of real number and floating point arithmetic.

3.1 Bits, Bytes and Words

Because of the two-state nature of logic gates, the natural way of representing information inside an electronic computer is by using the digits 0 and 1 called binary digits. A *binary digit* or *bit* is the basic unit from which all information is structured. Computers store and process information using groups of bits called *words*, as illustrated in figure 3.1.

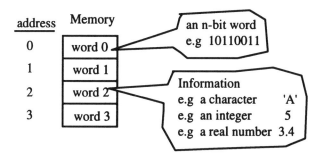

Figure 3.1 Words stored in memory

In principle, the number of bits in the group or *wordlength* can be any size, but for practical reasons modern computers currently standardise on multiples of 8-bits, typical wordlengths being 16, 32 or 64 bits. A group of 8 bits is called a *byte* so we can use this unit to express these wordlengths as 2 bytes, 4 bytes and 8 bytes respectively. Bytes are also used as the base unit for describing memory storage capacity, the symbols K, M and G being used to represent multiples of this unit as shown in the following table.

multiple	pronounced	symbol
1024	kilo	K
1024 × 1024	mega	M
1024 × 1024 × 1024	giga	G

Thus K or KB represents 1024 bytes, M or MB represents 1,048,576 bytes and G or GB represents 1,073,741,824 bytes.

3.2 Binary Codes

With an n-bit word there are 2^n different unique bit patterns that can be used to represent information. For example, if $n = 2$, there are 2^2 or four bit patterns 00, 01, 10 and 11. To each pattern we can assign some meaning, such as:

$$00 = \text{North, } 01 = \text{South, } 10 = \text{East, } 11 = \text{West}$$

The process of assigning a meaning to a set of bit patterns defines a particular *binary code*.

TQ 3.1   How many different 'things' can we represent with 7 bits ?

---

(1) ASCII Code

The *ASCII code* (American Standard Code for Information Interchange), is a 7-bit character code originally adopted for representing a set of 128 different symbols that were needed for exchanging information between computers. These symbols include *alphanumeric* characters such as (A-Z, a-z, 0-9), special symbols such as (+,−,&,%,etc), and *control* characters including 'Line Feed' and 'Carriage Return'. Table 3.1 illustrates some of the printable ASCII codes such as 'A' = 1000001 and '%' = 0100101.

Table 3.1 ASCII codes for, 'A', 'z', '2' and '%'

Character	ASCII codes						
	b_6	b_5	b_4	b_3	b_2	b_1	b_0
A	1	0	0	0	0	0	1
z	1	1	1	1	0	1	0
2	0	1	1	0	0	1	0
%	0	1	0	0	1	0	1

$b_6, b_5, ... b_0$ are the seven bit positions, numbered from left to right.

Control codes, such as 'Carriage Return' = 0001101 and 'Line Feed' = 0001010, are called *non-printing* characters. The full ASCII table is given in Appendix 1.

In addition to providing a code for information exchange, the ASCII code has also been adapted for representing characters inside a computer. Normally characters occupy a single byte of memory: the lower 7 bits being used to represent the ASCII code and the upper bit being set to 0 or 1, depending upon the machine. The extra bit can also be used to provide additional codes for storing graphic characters, or as a *parity bit* for checking single bit errors.

TQ 3.2   By referring to the ASCII table in Appendix 1, write down the ASCII codes for the characters 'a', 'Z' and '*'.

Binary codes can also be used to represent other entities, such as instructions and numbers. To represent numeric data we require a set of rules or *numbering system* for assigning values to the codes.

3.3 Number Systems

(1) Decimal number system

We represent decimal numbers using strings of digits taken from the set, {9,8,7,6,5,4,3,2,1,0}. Moving from right to left, each symbol represents a linearly increasing value. To represent numbers greater than 9 we use combinations of digits and apply a *weighting* to each digit according to its position in the number. For example, the decimal *integer* 126 is assigned a value of:

$$1 \times 100 + 2 \times 10 + 6 \times 1 = 100 + 20 + 6$$

The weighting applied to these digits is 10 raised to the power of the position of the digit, as shown in figure 3.2.

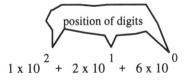

$$1 \times 10^{2} + 2 \times 10^{1} + 6 \times 10^{0}$$

Figure 3.2 Weightings used in the decimal number system

The position of a digit is found by counting from right to left starting at position 0.

Fractional or *real* numbers use a decimal point to separate negative powers of 10 from positive powers of ten. For example 52.6 represents:

$$5 \times 10^1 + 2 \times 10^0 + 6 \times 10^{-1}$$

The reason for using 10 is that there are ten different digits in this representation, which we call the *base* or *radix* of the system. Other positional number systems use different sets of digits and therefore have different bases. To distinguish one number system from another, we often subscript the number by its base, such as $126_{10.}$

(2) Binary number system

The binary number system uses just two digits {0,1} and therefore has a base of 2. The positional weighting of the digits is based on powers of 2, giving the number 1011_2 for example, a decimal value of:

$$1 \times 2^3 + 0 \times 2^2 + 1 \times 2^1 + 1 \times 2^0 = 8 + 0 + 2 + 1 = 11_{10}$$

This system of weighting is called *purebinary*, the binary digit furthest to the right being the *least significant bit* (lsb) and the one furthest to the left being the *mostsignificant bit* (msb).

TQ 3.3   What is the decimal value of the number 11.1_2?

---

(3) Hexadecimal number system

The hexadecimal (Hex) number system is a base-16 system and therefore has 16 different symbols to represent its digits. By convention the symbols adopted are {0,1,2,3,4,5,6,7,8,9,A,B,C,D,E,F}, where:

$$A = 10_{10}, B = 11_{10}, C = 12_{10}, D = 13_{10}, E = 14_{10} \text{ and } F = 15_{10}$$

In this system the weighting is 16 raised to the power of the position of the digit. For example $A1F_{16}$ has a decimal value of:

$$A \times 16^2 + 1 \times 16^1 + F \times 16^0 = 10 \times 256 + 1 \times 16 + 15 \times 1 = 2591_{10}$$

(4) Binary to hexadecimal conversion

Table 3.2 compares the first sixteen digits of the binary number system with the hexadecimal number system.

Table 3.2 Comparison of binary and hexadecimal number systems

binary	hexadecimal
0000	0
0001	1
0010	2
0011	3
0100	4
0101	5
0110	6
0111	7
1000	8
1001	9
1010	A
1011	B
1100	C
1101	D
1110	E
1111	F

From the table we can see that a single hexadecimal digit is capable of representing a 4-bit binary number. Because of this fact, we can convert a binary number into hexadecimal by grouping the digits into 4's, replacing each group by one hexadecimal digit, as shown below:

$$\underline{1\,0\,1\,1\ \ 0\,0\,1\,1\ \ 1\,0\,1\,0}$$
$$\text{B} \qquad 3 \qquad \text{A}$$

The binary number 101100111010_2 expressed in hexadecimal is therefore $B3A_{16}$.

To convert a hexadecimal number into binary, we reverse this operation and replace each hexadecimal digit by a 4-bit binary number.

TQ 3.4   Convert the hexadecimal number $ABCD_{16}$ into binary.

3.4 Negative Numbers

The binary system described so far is unable to represent negative integers and for this reason we call it *unsigned* binary. To support the use of negative numbers it is necessary to modify our representation to include information about the sign as well as the magnitude of a number. In this section we will consider two ways of doing this.

(1) Sign and magnitude representation

In this representation, the leftmost bit of the number is used as a *sign bit* and the remaining bits are used to give its magnitude. By convention, 0 is used for positive numbers and 1 for negative numbers. For example, using an 8-bit representation the numbers -5_{10} and $+20_{10}$ are 10000101 and 00010100 respectively.

TQ 3.5   What do 10001111 and 01010101 represent?

Unfortunately, representing numbers in this way makes binary addition and subtraction, which is performed by the Arithmetic and Logic Unit (ALU), more awkward to deal with. When performing addition for example, the sign bits must be checked before the magnitudes are separated out and added. If the sign bits are different, then a binary subtraction must be substituted for an addition, and before completing the operation, an appropriate sign bit must be reinserted. These extra processing steps add to the complexity of the ALU and increases the execution time of the operation.

TQ 3.6   How is zero represented in this system?

---

(2) Two's complement representation
In this representation there is only one representation of zero and it is more flexible than sign and magnitude in that it allows binary addition and subtraction to be treated in the same way. Rather than separating the sign from the magnitude, the 'negativeness' of the number is built into it. This is accomplished by giving the most significant bit position of an n-bit number a weighting of -2^{n-1} instead of $+2^{n-1}$ that we use with unsigned binary. Therefore with an 8-bit representation, the numbers $+127_{10}$ and -127_{10} are given by:

$$+127 = 01111111 = -0{\times}2^7 + 1{\times}2^6 + 1{\times}2^5 + 1{\times}2^4 + 1{\times}2^3 + 1{\times}2^2 + 1{\times}2^1 + 1{\times}2^0$$
$$-127 = 10000001 = -1{\times}2^7 + 0{\times}2^6 + 0{\times}2^5 + 0{\times}2^4 + 0{\times}2^3 + 0{\times}2^2 + 0{\times}2^1 + 1{\times}2^0$$

We can visualise these two numbers as shown in figure 3.3, where the most significant bit provides a large negative contribution and the remaining seven bits provide a positive contribution.

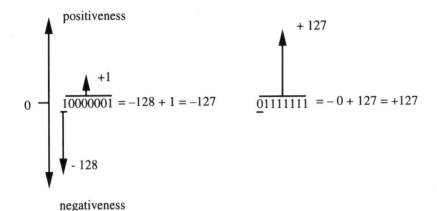

Figure 3.3 Showing the weighting of two's complement numbers

Any two's complement number where the most significant bit (msb) is equal to 1, must have an overall negative value. The msb therefore acts as both a sign bit and a magnitude bit.

With an 8-bit two's complement representation, we can represent numbers between -128_{10} and $+127_{10}$ as shown in table 3.3.

Table 3.3 8-bit two's complement representation

−128	10000000
−127	10000001
−126	10000010
−2	11111110
−1	11111111
0	00000000
+1	00000001
+2	00000010
+126	01111110
+127	01111111

TQ 3.7   What would the number 10000111 represent?

From the table we can identify a connection between the bit pattern of a positive number, such as $+2 = 00000010$, and the bit pattern of its opposite number, $-2 = 11111110$. If we reverse all the bits of the number $+2$, exchanging '1' bits for '0' bits and vice versa, we get the bit pattern 11111101. This is called finding the *one's complement*. If we now add '1' to the lsb of this number and we get:

$$\begin{array}{r} 11111101\ + \\ \underline{1} \\ \underline{11111110} \end{array} = \text{two's complement}$$

TQ 3.8   What is the two's complement representation of the number -3_{10}?

Worked Example
What is the decimal value of the two's complement number 11110000 ?

Solution
Because the sign bit is 1, we know that it must be a negative number. If we represent this number as $-X$, then by its two's complement must be $-(-X) = +X$. The two's complement of 11110000 is 00010000 as shown below:

$$\begin{array}{r} 00001111\ + \\ \underline{1} \\ \underline{00010000} \end{array}$$

Because this is $+16_{10}$ then the decimal value of 11110000 is -16_{10}

3.5 Binary Arithmetic

(1) Binary addition

The rules for adding pairs of binary digits are given in table 3.4. Using these rules, we add the binary numbers 1010 and 0011 by adding the digits together in pairs, starting with the least significant pair of digits on the far right, as shown in the following example.

$$\begin{array}{r} 1\ 0\ 1\ 0\ + \\ \underline{0\ 0\ 1\ 1} \\ \underline{1\ 1\ 0\ 1} \\ 1 \end{array}$$

Table 3.4 Rules for binary addition

digits added		Sum	carry-out
0 + 0		0	0
0 + 1		1	0
1 + 0		1	0
1 + 1		0	1

Notice how the carry-out generated when adding the second pair of digits gets included as a carry-in to the sum of the next most significant pair of digits, just as we do with decimal addition. Table 3.5 makes this more explicit and shows how the sum (S) and carry-out (C_o) depend upon the digits (A and B) being added and the carry-in (C_i).

Table 3.5 Rules for binary addition with carry-in included

A	B	C_i		S	C_o
0	0	0		0	0
0	1	0		1	0
1	0	0		1	0
1	1	0		0	1
0	0	1		1	0
0	1	1		0	1
1	0	1		0	1
1	1	1		1	1

If you look back at the truth-table for a full-adder, given in §2.2, you will see that it is exactly the same as Table 3.5. We can therefore perform binary addition electronically using a chain of full-adders, as shown below.

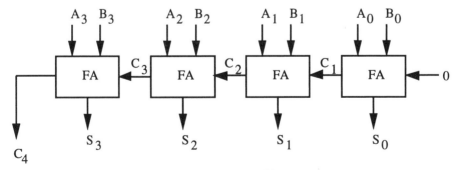

Figure 3.4 4-bit binary adder circuit

This circuit is suitable for adding two 4-bit numbers, denoted as $A_3 A_2 A_1 A_0$ and $B_3 B_2 B_1 B_0$, the sum being given by $S_3 S_2 S_1 S_0$. The carry-out from each stage provides a carry-in to its adjacent stage, so that it gets included when adding the next most-significant pairs of bits. The final carry-out, C_4, is 1 if the sum exceeds four bits and is 0 otherwise.

TQ 3.9 Why is the carry-in to the first stage of the adder set to 0?

This type of circuit would form part of the ALU, the data to be added being held in special registers during the operation. After the operation, the sum $S_3 S_2 S_1$ S_0 would also be stored in a register, together with information about its condition, such as the value of C_4. Conditions are recorded by setting and clearing *flags* in a Condition Code Register (CCR).

(2) Two's complement arithmetic

We add two's complement numbers in the same way as we add unsigned binary. For example, $12 + 20 = 32$ as shown below.

$$
\begin{array}{rl}
12 = & 00001100 \; + \\
20 = & \underline{00010100} \\
     & \underline{00100000} = 32
\end{array}
$$

We can also add negative numbers, such as $-1 + (-2) = -3$, provided that we ignore the bit carried-out of the sum.

$$
\begin{array}{rl}
-1 = & 11111111 \; + \\
-2 = & \underline{11111110} \\
     & \underline{11111101} = -3
\end{array}
$$
(ignore) 1↵

If we add large positive or large negative numbers together, we sometimes get the wrong answers, as the following examples illustrate.

$$
\begin{array}{rl}
64 = & 01000000 \; + \\
65 = & \underline{01000001} \\
     & \underline{10000001} = -127 \; \text{(should be +129 !)}
\end{array}
$$

$$
\begin{array}{rl}
-64 = & 11000000 \; + \\
-65 = & \underline{10111111} \\
      & \underline{01111111} = +127 \; \text{(should be} - 129 \; \text{!)}
\end{array}
$$
(ignore) 1↵

These are examples of *arithmetic overflow*, which occurs whenever a sum exceeds the range of the representation. In the first example, the sum should be +129 and in the second it should be −129. From table 3.3, we can see that these results are both out of range, because the largest and smallest numbers that can be represented are +127 and −128. Overflow is a consequence of two's complement arithmetic and can only occur when we add two numbers of the same sign. If the sign bit of the sum is different from that of the numbers being added, then overflow has taken place. The ALU signals this event by setting the *overflow flag* in the Condition Code Register.

One of the main advantages in using a two's complement representation, is that the ALU can perform binary subtraction using addition. For example, 7−5 is the same as 7+(−5), so to perform this operation we *add* 7 to the two's complement of 5. This is shown below.

$$
\begin{array}{r}
00000111\ + \\
11111010 \\
1 \\
\hline
00000010 = +2_{10}
\end{array}
$$

(ignore) $1\lrcorner$

To perform this type of operation electronically we can use the circuit shown in figure 3.5. The 8-bit numbers to be subtracted, $B_7....B_0$ and $A_7....A_0$ are applied as inputs to the chain of full-adders, the one's complement of $B_7....B_0$ being produced using NOT-gates. The carry-in to the first stage of the circuit is set to 1 and the difference $D_7....D_0$, is produced at the output.

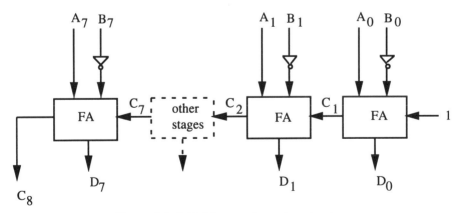

Figure 3.5 8-bit binary subtraction circuit

TQ 3.10   Why is the carry-in of the first stage set to 1?

3.6 Binary Coded Decimal (BCD)

When entering decimal data into a computer, the data must be converted into some binary form before processing can begin. To reduce the time needed to perform this conversion, we sometimes use a less compact but easily converted form of binary representation called Binary Coded Decimal (BCD).

To convert a decimal number into BCD, we use a 4-bit positional code for each decimal digit. It is usual to weight these digits in the normal 8-4-2-1 way, so that the decimal digits 1, 2, 3,... are replaced by the BCD codes 0001, 0010, 0011,.... Figure 3.6 illustrates how the decimal number 9164 is encoded and stored in two consecutive bytes of memory

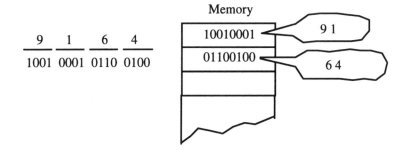

Figure 3.6 BCD representation of decimal number 9164

TQ 3.11   Which 4-bit binary codes are left unused by the BCD representation?

Because of these unused or *invalid codes*, we cannot perform arithmetic on BCD numbers in the same way as we do with pure binary. For example, 9+1 would give 1010, which is an invalid code. To overcome this problem most microprocessors include special logic in the ALU for performing BCD or *decimal* arithmetic.

3.7 Floating Point Representation

In the decimal number system we frequently represent very large or very small numbers in *scientific notation* rather than as a fixed point number. For example, the fixed point decimal numbers 299800000 and 0.0000000000000000001602 can be represented as $2.998 \times 10^{+8}$ and 1.602×10^{-19} respectively. The power to which 10 is raised, such as +8 or −19, is called the *exponent* or *characteristic*, while the number in front is called the *mantissa*.

By substituting the base 2 for the base 10, we can use a similar notation for representing real numbers in a computer. For example, the decimal number 5.625

could be represented as 1.01101×2^2 or 1011.01×2^{-1}, where each exponent specifies the true position of the binary point relative to its current position in the mantissa. Because the binary point can be dynamically altered by adjusting the size of the exponent, we call this representation *floating point*.

(1) Storing floating point numbers

To store a floating point number we need to record information about the sign and magnitude of both the mantissa and the exponent. The number of words used to do this and the way this information is encoded is called a *floating point format*. Figure 3.7 shows how 1.011010×2^2 might be represented and stored using two bytes or 16-bits of storage space.

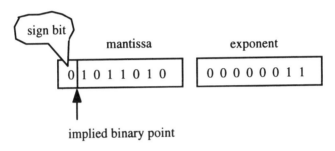

Figure 3.7 A simple floating point format

With this particular format, a sign and magnitude representation is used for storing the mantissa and a two's complement representation is used for the exponent. Before storing this number it must be *normalised* by adjusting the exponent so that the binary point is immediately before the most significant digit. The normalised form of the number 1.011010×2^2 is therefore given by $.1011010 \times 2^3$, so the digits 1011010 and the two's complement representation of the exponent +3, which is 00000011, are stored in their respective bytes.

TQ 3.12 What is the largest number we can represent using this format?

The *range* of numbers we can represent with an 8-bit exponent is approximately 10^{-39} to 10^{+39} and the *precision* we get with a 7-bit mantissa is about 1 part in 10^3. We can increase the precision by using more bits to store the mantissa, but with a 16-bit mode of representation, this can only be done by reducing the range. To overcome this type of problem, most machines support two modes of precision, *single precision* and *double precision*, as illustrated in figure 3.8.

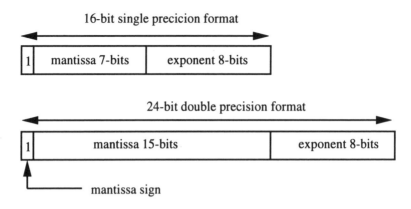

Figure 3.8   Single and double precision formats

TQ 3.13   How would the number 5.125_{10} be stored in single precision format?

---

(2) Floating point arithmetic

Floating point arithmetic is more complicated than integer arithmetic. To illustrate this, we will consider the steps involved in performing the operation 5.125 + 13.625, using single precision arithmetic. We will assume that these numbers have been normalised and stored in memory, as shown in figure 3.9(a).

The first step in this operation involves aligning the binary points of the two numbers, which is carried out by comparing their exponents and arithmetically shifting the smaller number until its exponent matches that of the other. In figure 3.9(b), the mantissa of the smaller number 5.125, is shifted one place to the right so that its exponent becomes the same as that of the number 13.625. Notice that a zero has been inserted in its most significant bit position.

Having the same exponents, the sign bits are separated and the mantissae are added, as shown in figure 3.9(c). Because the result now occupies 8 bits, it must be *renormalised* , by shifting the bits one place to the right and incrementing the exponent. Finally, the sign bit is reinserted as shown in figure 3.9(d), to produce a sum of $+ 0.1001011 \times 2^5$ or 18.75_{10}.

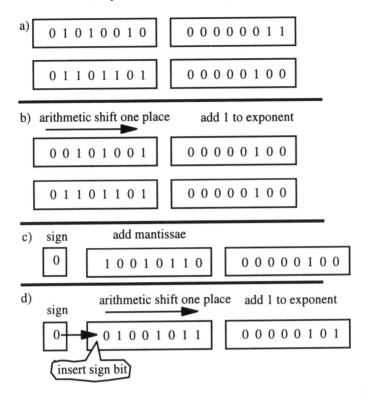

Figure 3.9 Floating point addition

Floating point multiplication and division operations also involve a number of steps including adding/subtracting the exponents, multiplying/dividing the mantissae and renormalising the result. These operations can be carried out either by using software routines or by employing special hardware in the form of a floating point *coprocessor*. Floating point or numeric coprocessors improve the performance of compute intensive applications, by allowing any floating-point arithmetic to take place in parallel with the CPU. When the CPU detects a floating point instruction, the operands are passed to the coprocessor, which performs the arithmetic operation while the CPU proceeds with another activity.

3.8 Summary

Computers store and manipulate information as n-bit words. An n-bit word can represent 2^n different entities, such as characters and numbers. A group of 8 bits is called a byte and can be used to store a single ASCII character. The binary number system uses a positional weighting scheme based on powers of 2. The hexadecimal number systems uses a positional weighting based on powers of 16. The hexadecimal number system provides a useful shorthand for representing large binary numbers. Negative numbers are often represented in binary form using the two's complement representations. This representation allows subtraction to be carried out using the same basic circuitry used for addition. When adding two's complement numbers with the same sign, a condition called overflow can occur. An overflow condition is automatically flagged in the Condition Code Register. Real numbers can be represented as floating point numbers. Floating point numbers use a particular format to represent the mantissa and the exponent. Floating point arithmetic involves more steps than with integer arithmetic and can be performed using either software routines or by employing additional hardware in the form of a coprocessor. Floating point coprocessors can execute floating point operations in parallel with the CPU.

3.9 Answers to Text Questions

TQ 3.1   With n = 7 there are $2^7 = 128$ unique bit patterns that can be used to represent different 'things'

TQ 3.2   'a' = 1100001, 'Z' = 1011010 and '*' = 0101010

TQ 3.3 $1 \times 2^1 + 1 \times 2^0 + 1 \times 2^{-1} = 2 + 1 + 0.5 = 3.5_{10}$

TQ 3.4   1010 1011 1100 1101

TQ 3.5   10001111 represents -15_{10} and 01010101 represents $+85_{10}$

TQ 3.6   Zero can be written as either 1000000 or 00000000

TQ 3.7   This number would represent $-128 + 7 = -121$

TQ 3.8   1. Write down the 8-bit representation of the number, $+3_{10}$
          00000011 and find its one's complement, 11111100
          2. Add 1 to the lsb

$$\begin{array}{r} 11111100 + \\ 1 \\ \hline 11111101 \end{array} = \text{two's complement}$$

TQ 3.9   Because there is no carry-in for the first pair of digits

TQ 3.10   To add 1 to the least significant bit position

TQ 3.11   Because only 10 of the 16 possible 4-bit binary codes are used, we are left with the six invalid codes.
          1010, 1011, 1100, 1101, 1110, 1111

TQ 3.12   The largest number is $+ 0.1111111 \times 2^{+127}$

TQ 3.13 $+5.125_{10} = 101.001 \times 2^0 = .101001 \times 2^{+3}$ when normalised. It would therefore be stored as:

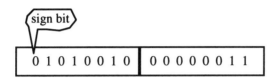

3.10 Exercises

1.   How many binary codes can we generate with 16 bits ?

2.   Convert the following decimal numbers into binary
        (a) 16 (b) 127   (c) 255

3.   Convert the following binary numbers into decimal
        (a) 0111   (b) 101101000011 (c) 1011.0111

4.   Convert the following numbers into hexadecimal
        (a) 101011101011 (b) 11100110 (c) 010100011

5.   Perform the following binary additions:
        (a) 00101 + 10110   (b) 100111 + 100101 + 000001

6.   If a byte addressable RAM occupies the hexadecimal addresses A000 to BFFF, then how many K of storage space is available?

7.   Perform the following operations using 8-bit two's complement arithmetic. In which cases will arithmetic overflow occur ?
        (a) 100 + 27 (b) 84 + 52 (c) 115 – 64 (d) –85 – 44

8.   Represent $+101.1111 \times 2^{+5}$ and $- 0.0001 \times 2^{+6}$ using the simple floating point format given in figure 3.7

References

Clements, A (1991), *The Principles of Computer Hardware*, Oxford University Press, pp. 141-220.

4   Fetching and Executing Instructions

At the heart of a microcomputer system lies the CPU or processor. The processor runs a program by repeatedly fetching and executing instructions from main memory. By using a step-by-step approach, this chapter outlines the way in which this is done using a highly simplified processor. This will provide a foundation for understanding the operation of a real processor in chapter 5.

4.1 Processor-Memory Interconnection

In a microcomputer system the processor is connected to main memory by a *data*, *address* and *control* bus, as shown in figure 4.1.

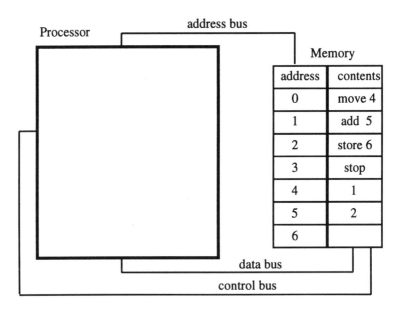

Figure 4.1 Showing the data, address and control buses

A program consists of a series of *instructions* or actions to be carried out by the processor. These actions are performed on data. Instructions and data are stored in primary or main memory during program execution. In figure 4.1, instructions and data occupy various memory locations, each location being identified by a unique *address*.

4.2 Fetching Instructions

When running a program, the processor fetches instructions by providing an address on the address bus and reading the instruction from the data bus. To carry out this task, the processor uses a number of *internal registers*, as shown in figure 4.2.

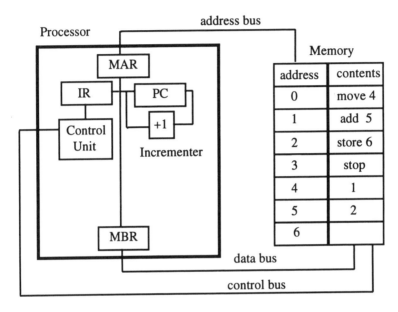

Figure 4.2 Showing the MAR, MBR, IR and PC registers

A register is a small high speed memory location used for the temporary storage of data or control information. There are four registers shown in the figure: a *Memory Address Register* (MAR); a *Memory Buffer Register* (MBR); an *Instruction Register* (IR); and a *Program Counter* (PC). The registers are connected together by an internal data path or *bus*. The flow of data along this bus is managed by the *Control Unit* (CU). To understand the purpose of these registers, we will examine how the first instruction in the program, *move 4*, is fetched.

Before running a program, the PC must be initialised with the address of the first instruction. This happens to be address 0 for the program shown in the figure. The *instruction cycle* begins when the address stored in the PC is transferred along the processor's internal data bus into the MAR, as shown in figure 4.3.

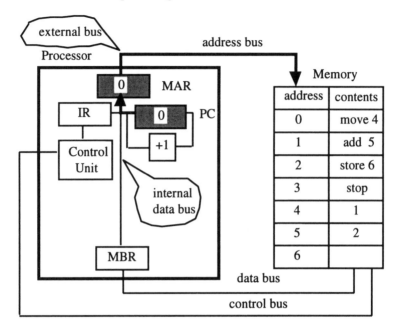

Figure 4.3 Showing the operation [MAR] ← [PC]

We can represent this operation by the *Register Transfer Language* statement:

$$[MAR] \leftarrow [PC]$$

The Register Transfer Language or RTL statement reads as follows:

"the contents of "	[ ]
"the program counter register"	PC
"replace"	←
"the contents of "	[ ]
"the memory address register"	MAR

RTL is a concise way of describing the movement of information through the system.

The MAR provides an *interface* between the processor's internal bus and the external address bus. Once in the MAR, the instruction address is passed along the address bus to the memory unit. As mentioned in chapter 1, a bus provides an electrical path to carry information from one unit to another. Having made this transfer, the PC is incremented. This is illustrated in figure 4.4.

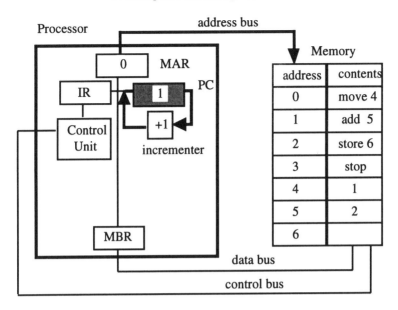

Figure 4.4 Showing the operation [PC] ← [PC] + 1

The RTL statement for this operation is:

$$[PC] \leftarrow [PC] + 1$$

TQ 4.1   Describe the meaning of this RTL statement.

The PC now contains 0 + 1 = 1, which is the address of the next instruction, *add 5*. This allows the CPU to keep track of where it is in the program.

As the memory unit decodes the address provided on the address bus and locates the *memory cell* containing the instruction, the processor generates a *read signal* on the *control bus*. The memory unit responds by placing a copy of the contents of this memory location on the data bus, as shown in figure 4.5. This is the contents of memory address 0, which is the instruction *move 4*.

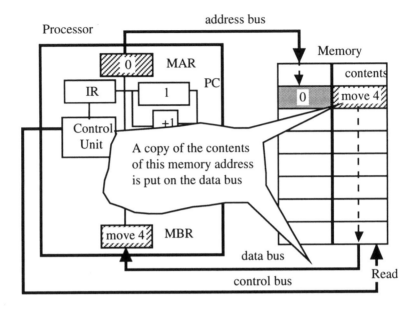

Fig 4.5 Showing the operation [MBR] ← [M([MAR])]

This instruction is now copied from the data bus and *latched* in to the MBR. We represent this phase of the instruction cycle by the RTL statement:

$$[MBR] \leftarrow [M([MAR])]$$

which reads:

"the contents of the MAR"	[MAR]
"provide an address for"	([MAR])
"the memory unit, M"	M([MAR])
"whose contents"	[M([MAR])]
"replace"	←
"the contents of the MBR	[MBR]

TQ 4.2   What is the value of [M(0)]?

The MBR *interfaces* the processor's internal bus to the external data bus.

Having *buffered* a copy of the instruction into the MBR, the processor now transfers the instruction along its internal data bus into the IR, as shown in figure 4.6.

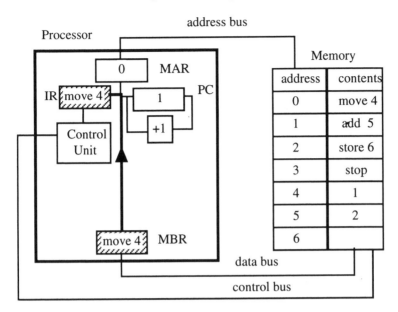

*Figure 4.6 Showing **move 4** being transferred into the Instruction Register*

TQ 4.3   Represent this stage of the operation using RTL.

Once in the IR, the instruction is decoded by the *Control Unit* (CU). The CU generates a sequence of *control signals* from information provided by the instruction's *operation code* (opcode), as shown in figure 4.7. This phase of the instruction cycle is represented by the RTL statement:

$$CU \leftarrow [IR(opcode)]$$

Control signals are used to initiate events, such as the movement of data between registers. The type and order of events varies from one instruction to another. To generate sequences of such events, a timing reference source or *clock* is used. The clock unit shown in figure 4.7, provides the CU with this high frequency *clock signal.*

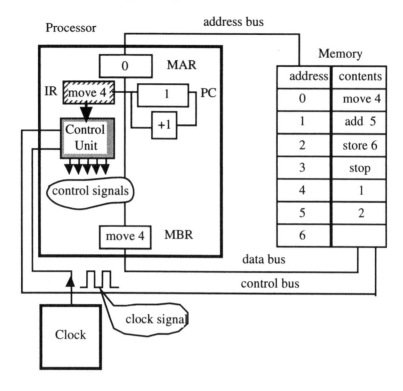

*Figure 4.7 Showing the **move 4** instruction being decoded*

This completes the *fetch* part of the instruction cycle, this phase being the same for all instructions. Following this, the processor enters an *execute* phase, which varies according to the type of operation specified in the instruction. Before we examine the execution phase of *move 4*, we need to describe the *format* of our instructions.

4.3 Instruction Format

(1) Machine instructions

In chapter 3, we mentioned that instructions are stored and manipulated by a computer in binary form. For example, the instruction we have symbolically represented as *move 4* might have a binary form 1011001000000100, which we call *machine code*. Logically, this instruction is composed of two fields, as shown in figure 4.8(a). These fields are called the *opcode* and the *operand address*. The opcode specifies the type of operation the processor is to perform, while the address of the data or *operand* is specified by the operand address. The format of the *move 4* instruction is shown in figure 4.8(b).

The first byte is a binary code for the operation *move* and specifies that the processor is to move data into its data register. The second byte is the *address* of the data to be moved, which is decimal address *4*.

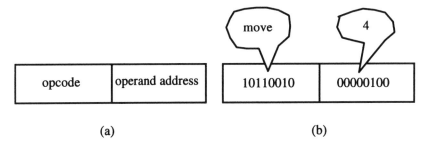

| opcode | operand address | 10110010 | 00000100 |

(a)   (b)

Figure 4.8 Simple instruction format

TQ 4.4   How many different opcodes can we represent with 8 bits?

Although each pattern could be used to represent a different instruction, in practice, some instructions use several *addressing modes*, each mode being identified by a different opcode.

With this limited 16-bit format, it has only been possible to include one 8-bit operand field. We therefore call these *one-address* instructions. Because our processor has no facilities for calculating addresses, the operand field is only used to hold the actual or *absolute* address of the operand. In other words, the processor only supports one form of *addressing mode*. Real processors often allow more than one operand to be specified in an instruction and also support several different addressing modes. We will discuss the addressing modes of a real processor in §5.3.

(2) Assembly language instructions

When writing a program for a particular processor, it is easier to write and under-stand programs when the instructions are represented symbolically, such as *move 4*, rather than when they are written in machine code. For this reason, most *low-level language* programs are written in *assembly language*.

An assembly language instruction has a *mnemonic* to represent the opcode, such as *move*, and symbols to specify operand addresses, such as *4*. If registers are used to specify operands, then these are also included. After writing a program in assembly language, each instruction must be translated into machine code before the program can be loaded into memory and executed by the processor. This is carried out by a program called an *assembler*.

4.4 Executing Instructions

To support instruction execution, our simple processor uses an 8-bit *Data Register* (D0) and an *Arithmetic and Logic Unit* (ALU), as shown in figure 4.9. As we mentioned in chapter 3, the ALU is a logic block which performs a limited number of arithmetic and logic operations, such as '+', '−', 'AND', etc. Our ALU operates upon data that has been stored in D0 or which has been buffered in the MBR. After performing such an operation, the content of D0 is overwritten with any results produced.

(1) Executing move 4

Having decoded the opcode *move* as, "move data from memory into the data register D0", the CU begins the instruction execution phase by generating control signals to perform the following actions:

1. [MAR] ← [IR(operand address)]

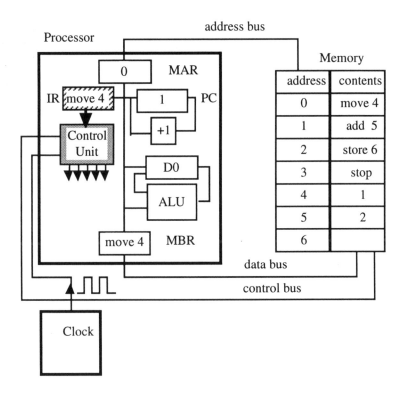

Figure 4.9 Showing the ALU and Data Register D0

This operation transfers the operand address into the MAR, as shown in figure 4.10. The CU then performs a memory read operation in the usual way, buffering a copy of the contents of memory address *4* into the MBR:

2. [MBR] ← [M(4)]

To complete the execution of this instruction, the CU transfers the operand from the MBR in to D0:

3. [D0] ← [MBR]

These stages are also shown in figure 4.10.

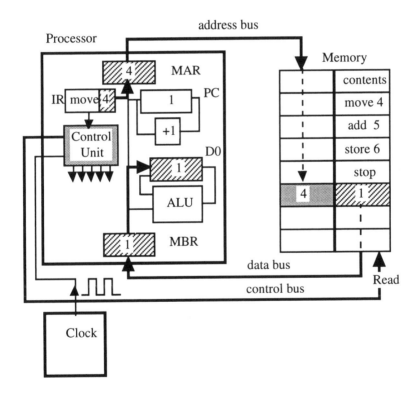

Figure 4.10 Showing the three steps involved when executing **move 4**

Having fetched and executed this instruction, the processor begins another instruction cycle. This cycle of fetching and executing instructions is called the *fetch-execute cycle*, and is repeated until the program is terminated in some way. In our simple program, this is accomplished using a special instruction called *stop*.

TQ 4.5   Using RTL, describe the fetch phase of the next instruction cycle.

---

(2) Executing add 5

During decoding, the opcode of the instruction *add*, is interpreted as "add the contents of a memory address to the data stored in D0", the data register D0 being *implied* by the opcode. Because the memory address is contained in the operand address, instruction execution begins with the operation:

> 1. [MAR] ← [IR(operand address)]

This is followed by a memory read operation to fetch the operand:

> 2. [MBR] ← [M(5)]

The operands to be added are now in D0 and the MBR, as shown in figure 4.11(a). To perform the addition, a control signal from the CU is used to set the ALU into the addition mode, which has been denoted by a "+" sign inside the ALU. The operands are then transferred into the ALU, as shown in figure 4.11(b) and which we can represent by:

> 3. ALU ← [D0]
>   ALU ← [MBR]

These operations occur in *parallel*, because the operands are moved along separate internal data paths.

Once in the ALU the data is added and the result, $1 + 2 = 3$, is deposited back into the data register D0, as shown in figure 4.11(c). We represent this operation by:

> 4. [D0] ← ALU

The processor records information on the outcome of this operation in a *Condition Code Register* (CCR), by setting or clearing certain bits or *flags*. For example, because the result 3 is a non-zero number, the ALU clears the zero bit or Z-flag in the CCR.

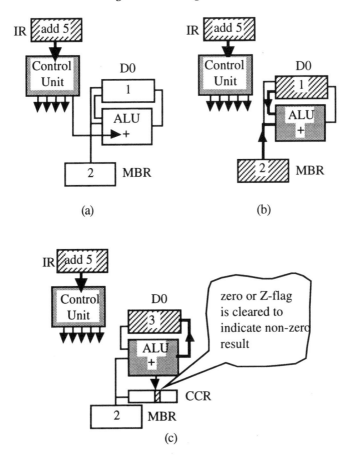

Fig 4.11 Showing the ALU during an add operation

TQ 4.6   How would the carry flag, that we described in §3.5, be affected?

This completes the fetch-execute cycle for the instruction *add 5*. The third instruction in our program, *store 6*, is now fetched in the usual way.

(3) Executing store 6

During decoding *store 6* is interpreted as, 'store the contents of data register D0 in a memory address 6'. The CU responds with the following operations:

$$[MAR] \leftarrow [IR(\text{operand address})]$$
$$[MBR] \leftarrow [D0]$$
$$[M(6)] \leftarrow [MBR]$$

TQ 4.7   What do you think the operation [M(6)] ← [MBR] represents?

This last operation involves the generation of a *write signal* on the control bus, as shown in figure 4.12.

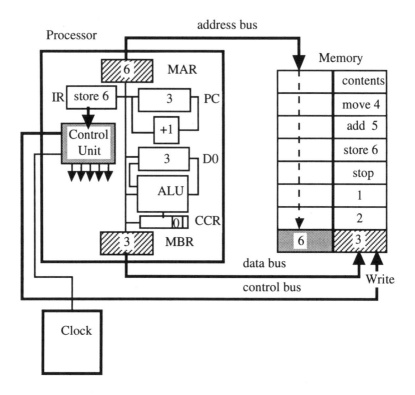

Figure 4.12 Showing a memory write operation

Having completed the execution of instruction *store 6*, the processor fetches and executes the final instruction in the program, *stop*. As mentioned earlier, this instruction halts any further execution of the program.

4.5 Summary

Programs are executed by repeatedly fetching instructions from Memory in to the processor and then executing them. This is called the fetch-execute cycle. Three buses are used to exchange information with the Memory Unit: an Address Bus, a Data Bus and a Control Bus. To organise this flow of instructions, the processor uses a number of special purpose registers: a Program Counter, an Instruction Register, a Memory Address Register and a Memory Buffer Register.

Instruction decoding is performed by the Control Unit, which generates appropriate control signals in response to the opcode of the instruction. The operand field is used to specify the address of any data required by the instruction. An ALU is used to carry out arithmetic and logic operations on data, temporarily stored in a Data Register or passed to it from the MBR. A Condition Code Register is used to record details about the result of the operation by setting and clearing flags.

4.6 Answers to Text Questions

TQ 4.1   The contents of the program counter, plus one, replaces the contents of the program counter.

TQ 4.2   M(0) is the memory location whose address is 0.
[M(0)] is the contents of memory location 0 or instruction *move 4*.

TQ 4.3   [IR] ← [MBR]

TQ 4.4   The number of unique bit patterns or opcodes we can represent with 8 bits is 2^8 or 256.

TQ 4.5   [MAR]   ← [PC]
          [PC]   ← [PC] + 1
          [MBR]   ← [M(1)]
          [IR]   ← [MBR]
          CU   ← [IR(opcode)]

TQ 4.6   There would be no carry and therefore the carry flag would be cleared.

TQ 4.7   The RTL statement, [M(6)] ← [MBR], represents a memory write operation, the operand being transferred from the MBR to address 6.

4.7 Exercises

1.   State the names and purposes of the following registers:
      PC, MBR, MAR, CCR.

2.   Complete the following RTL description of an instruction fetch cycle:
      [MAR]   ←   [ ]
      [ ]   ←   [PC] + 1
      [MBR]   ←   [M ( )]
      [ ]   ←   [MBR]

3.   What is the name of the bit marked Z in the CCR? How is it affected when a data register is loaded with zero?

4.   If an instruction was to modify the contents of the PC register, what affect would this have on the program?

5.   For a 16-bit processor with byte addressable memory, the fetch-cycle is modified to include:

$$[PC] \leftarrow [PC] + 2$$

Why is this?

6.   What is the difference between a machine code program and an assembly language program? How do we convert one to the other?

5 The Motorola MC68000

In this chapter we examine the *instruction set architecture* or programmer-visible aspects of a real processor, the Motorola MC68000. We begin by describing the register set, the types of instruction supported and some of the powerful addressing modes provided. This is followed by an overview of instruction formatting and coding. Towards the end of the chapter, we analyse a couple of assembly language programs and discuss the modes in which the 68000 can operate.

5.1 Programmer's Model of the 68000

From an assembly language programmer's point of view, a 68000 processor contains the special and general purpose registers shown in figure 5.1.

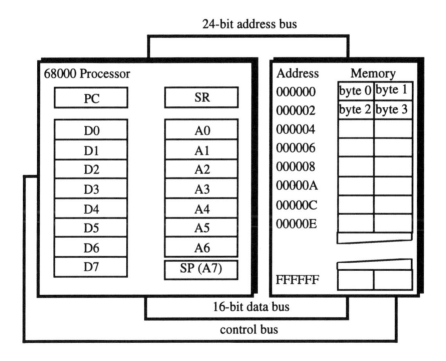

Figure 5.1 Model of the 68000

The processor is connected to memory by a control bus, a 16-bit data bus and a 24-bit address bus[1]. This allows 2^{24} or 16 Mbytes of byte addressable memory to be accessed, the addresses ranging from 000000_{16} to $FFFFFF_{16}$.

(1) Data registers

The registers D0 to D7 are 32-bit general purpose data registers, and are used for the temporary storage of operands. These registers can store three sizes of operand, Byte (8-bit), Word (16-bit) or Longword (32-bit). For example, the instruction:

$$\text{MOVE.B} \qquad \$0,D1$$

moves or copies an 8-bit operand (denoted by the suffix 'B'), from memory address 000000_{16} into data register D1, the dollar sign, '\$', being used to express the fact that the number which follows is to be treated as a hexadecimal value. The result of this operation is to place a copy of the byte stored in memory location 000000_{16} , which is byte 0 (see figure 5.1), into bit positions 0 to 7 of data register D1, as shown in figure 5.2.

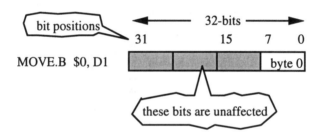

Figure 5.2 Showing the result of MOVE.B $0,D1

The higher order bits, 8 to 31, are unaffected, so that D1 is effectively acting as an 8-bit register in this case.

In RTL we can represent the action of MOVE.B \$0,D1 as:

$$[D1(0:7)] \qquad \leftarrow \qquad [M(0)]$$

To move an operand of size Word or Longword, we append the suffixes W and L to the instruction mnemonic, as illustrated in figure 5.3.

---

[1] Actually there are 23 address lines $A_{23},..,A_1$ with A_0 replaced by two strobe lines.

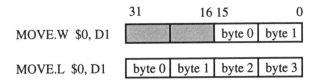

Figure 5.3 Illustrating word (W) and longword (L) operations

The instruction MOVE.W $0,D1 copies byte 0 and byte 1 into bit positions (0:15), leaving the higher order bits (16:31) unaffected, while MOVE.L $0,D1 replaces all bits in D1 with the bytes 0, 1, 2 and 3.

TQ 5.1   Write down an RTL description of MOVE.L $0,D1

In general, a two-operand instruction such as MOVE is written in the form:

OPERATION.S   <source>,<destination>

where the suffix 'S', specifies the size of the operand involved and where <source> and <destination> refer to the address of the *source* and *destination operands*. The source operand specifies the address of the data upon which the operation is to be performed, while the destination operand specifies the address where the result of the operation is to be placed. These might be memory locations or registers and are specified using various addressing modes. The allowable addressing modes depend upon the particular instruction.

TQ 5.2   What do you think the instruction MOVE.B D0,$6 does?

For an instruction like ADD.B D0,D1 which ADDs the lower byte contained in D0 to the lower byte contained in D1 and then puts the result in bit positions (0:7) of D1, the destination operand acts as both a source and a destination operand.

(2) Address registers

The eight 32-bit registers A0,..,A7 are *address registers* and are generally used for storing operand addresses. Address register A7 is used as a stack pointer (SP) which we shall describe in a moment. Unlike data registers, address registers can only be used for word and longword operations. They also differ from data registers in that all bits are affected by word operation and not just bits (0:15). For this reason, when moving data into an Address register a special type of move instruction, MOVEA, is provided. For example, the instruction:

MOVEA.L   #$89ABCDEF,A2

MOVEs the 32-bit *constant* or *literal* $89ABCDEF_{16}$ into address register A2, as shown in figure 5.4.

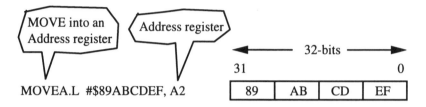

Figure 5.4 Showing the result of MOVEA.L #$89ABCDEF,A2

The hash sign, '#', is used to indicate that the source operand is specified using the immediate addressing mode. In this mode, the operand is contained as part of the instruction.

Worked Example
What would the instruction, MOVEA.L $89ABCDEF,A2 do?

Solution
This instruction copies the *contents* of memory address $ABCDEF_{16}$ into address register A2.
The most significant byte of the address, 89, plays no part in this because only 24 bits of the address are used to access memory.
In other words MOVEA.L $00ABCDEF,A2 does the same thing.

When copying a 16-bit literal into A2, using the instructions:

MOVEA.W #$7FFF, A2 or MOVEA.W #$8FFF, A2

the literal is treated as a signed value and is *sign extended* into bits (16:31) of the register, as shown in figure 5.5.

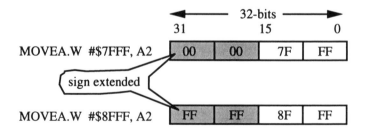

Figure 5.5 Sign extension when moving data to an Address Register

For the literal $7FFF_{16}$ or 0111111111111111_2, the most significant or *sign bit* is 0, which the 68000 extends into bits (0:31) of the register by storing $00007FFF_{16}$.

TQ 5.3   Why does the 68000 store $FFFF8FFF_{16}$ when moving $8FFF_{16}$ into address register A2?

---

(3) Stack Pointer

A stack is a data structure in which items are stored or *pushed* onto it in one order, such as *a,b,c* and then retrieved or *pulled* from it in the reverse order *c,b,a*. For this reason a stack is also called a Last In First Out (*LIFO*) list.

The 68000 implements a stack by using a segment of memory in conjunction with a register called a Stack Pointer (SP). The SP holds the address or points to the memory location of the last item pushed on the stack. This location is called the top of the stack. With the 68000, address register A7 is used for this purpose and is automatically used when saving the return addresses of subroutines. We will describe how the stack operates in one of the program examples given later in the chapter.

(4) Status Register

A diagram of the 16-bit Status Register (*SR*) is shown in figure 5.6. It is composed of two bytes, the *system byte* and the *user byte* or *Condition Code Register* (*CCR*). The CCR is similar to the one we described in chapter 4 and contains a number of flags which are automatically set/cleared by the ALU.

The system byte contains three *interrupt mask bits*, a *supervisor bit* (S) and a *trace bit* (T). The supervisor bit is set (S = 1), when the 68000 is in *supervisor mode* and cleared (S = 0), when in *user mode*. When the trace bit is set (T = 1), the 68000 is in *trace mode*. We will describe the supervisor and trace modes later in the chapter.

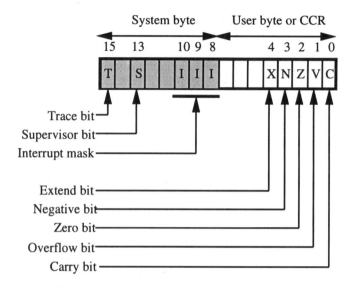

Figure 5.6 The MC68000 Status Register

(5) Program Counter

The Program Counter (PC) is used to keep track of the next program instruction to be executed. The 68000's PC is a 32-bit register, although only the lower 24 bits affect access to memory. Normally, instructions are executed sequentially, each instruction occupying between one and five consecutive words of memory (see §5.4). Instructions and multi-byte data must be stored at even addresses or *even byte boundaries*, otherwise the 68000 cannot access them and generates an error, by raising an *address exception*.

Branch or Jump instructions cause program control to pass to a non-sequential instruction by altering the content of the PC. This enables the processor to repeat sequences of instructions or to execute different sets of instructions depending on some condition in the CCR. We will describe examples of these instructions in the next section.

5.2 Instruction Types

The 68000 supports several different types of instruction, which can be grouped into classes. In this section, we will illustrate these classes with a selection of examples.

(1) Data movement instructions

These instructions allow data to be moved between registers, from one memory location to another or between a register and memory.

Examples

MOVE.W	D1,D2	MOVE or copy bits (0:15) of register D1 into bits (0:15) of D2.
MOVE.B	$100,$200	MOVE the byte stored in memory location $100, into memory location $200.
MOVE.L	D5,$200	MOVE bits (0:31) of D5 into memory from address $200 onwards.
MOVEQ	#7,D3	MOVE Quick, the constant 7 (sign extended) into bits (0:31) of D3. Note: −128 ≤ constant ≤ +127
LEA.L	$0010ABCD,A2	Load Effective Address $0010ABCD into address register A2.
SWAP	D7	Exchange the upper and lower 16-bit words of data register D7.

(2) Arithmetic and logic instructions

These instructions are used for integer arithmetic and Boolean operations: AND, OR, NOT and Exclusive OR.

Examples

ADD.B	D0,D1	ADD bits (0:7) in D0 to bits (0:7) in D1, leaving the result in D1.
SUBQ	#1,D0	SUBtract Quick the constant 1 from D0, leaving the result in D0. Note: 1 ≤ constant ≤ 8
ADDI.B	#7,$2000	ADD Immediate data constant 7 to the contents of memory location $2000, leaving the result in memory.

MULU	D1,D2	MULtiply the Unsigned 16-bit value D1(0:15) with D2(0:15), leaving the 32-bit longword result in D2.
NOT.B	D0	Invert bits (0:7) of D0.
AND.L	D0,D1	Perform the logical AND operation between each bit in D0 and its corresponding bit in D1. Leave result in D1.
ANDI.B	#1,D0	AND Immediate data constant 1 with bits (0:7) of D0, leaving result in D0.

Worked Example

If D0 contained zero, then what would be the result of ANDI.B #1,D0 ?

Solution

The bitwise AND between each bit in D0(0:7) and the immediate data bits is performed.

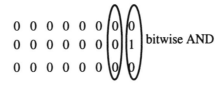

$$0\ 0\ 0\ 0\ 0\ 0\ 0\ 0$$
$$0\ 0\ 0\ 0\ 0\ 0\ 0\ 1\quad\text{bitwise AND}$$
$$0\ 0\ 0\ 0\ 0\ 0\ 0\ 0$$

From the truth-table of the AND function given in chapter 2, figure 2.2, the result of each bitwise operation is zero. In fact the only condition that would leave a non-zero result in D0 is if its least significant bit was set to 1. The fact that it is the least significant bit and not some other bit, is determined by the immediate data byte, which behaves as a *mask*.

---

(3) Bit manipulation instructions

These instructions are used for testing and operating upon single bits of an operand.

Examples

| BTST | #3,D7 | Test bit 3 of D7 and set the Z-flag in the CCR to reflect its value. |
| BCHG | #3,D7 | Test bit 3 of D7 and set the Z-flag to reflect its value. Then change the value of the bit. |

(4) Program control instructions

These instructions allow the processor to branch or jump from one part of a program to another, either unconditionally or depending upon the condition of the flags in the CCR.

Branch instructions

Examples

| BRA | LOOP | BRAnch unconditionally to the instruction labelled LOOP. |

| BEQ | LOOP | Branch to the instruction labelled LOOP on condition that the result of last instruction was Equal to zero, that is, $(Z = 1)$ in the CCR. |

Compare instructions

Compare instructions are used to explicitly update the flags in the CCR before a conditional branch instruction is encountered.

Examples

| CMP.W | D1,D0 | Subtract bits $(0:15)$ in D1 from bits $(0:15)$ in D0 and set the N, Z, V, C flags accordingly. The result is not stored and D0 is **not** modified. |

| CMPI.B | #$FF,D2 | Subtract the immediate data constant $FF from bits $(0:7)$ in D2 and set the N, Z, V, C flags accordingly. The result is not stored and D2 is **not** modified. |

Subroutine call/Return constructions

A subroutine is a sequence of instructions that can be called and executed from another program. The last instruction in a subroutine returns control back to the instruction immediately following the subroutine call instruction.

Examples

| BSR | ERR | The longword of the address immediately following the BSR instruction is pushed onto the system stack. Program execution then continues at the instruction labelled ERR. |

RTS   The return address is pulled from the system stack into
                       the PC allowing program execution to continue with the
                       instruction immediately following the subroutine call
                       instruction.

(5) Other instructions

There are a number of other instructions concerned with exception processing and
activities, such as stopping the processor, that do not fall into any of the above
classes. We will not attempt to describe these here, although interested readers
might like to study them by consulting the reference at the end of this chapter.

5.3 Addressing Modes

In chapter 4, we explained that an instruction is composed of an opcode and an
operand field which is used to specify the operand address. The 68000 supports
several methods of encoding the address of an operand, called *addressing modes*.

(1) Register Direct addressing

With this mode of addressing, the operand is held in either a data register or an
address register, as shown below.

Addressing mode	In the instruction	In a register	In memory
Register Direct		Dn	
(a) Data register (n between 0 and 7)		Operand	
		An	
(b) Address register (n between 0 and 7)		Operand	

Example

$$\text{MOVE.L} \qquad \text{A7,D5}$$

This instruction uses the *address register direct* addressing mode for its source
operand and the *data register direct* addressing mode for its destination operand.

(2) *Immediate addressing*

This addressing mode includes the actual operand as part of the instruction, as indicated below.

Addressing mode	In the instruction	In a register	In memory
Immediate	Operand		

The syntax used to indicate this addressing mode is #number or #symbol.

Examples

ADDI.B   #1,D0

This instruction uses immediate addressing to specify its source operand, which is the data constant or literal 1.

MOVEA.W   #TABLE,A2

This instruction uses immediate addressing to specify its source operand, which is the value of the symbolic name TABLE.

(3) *Absolute addressing*

With this addressing mode, the operand, which is stored in memory, is located by including the actual memory address of its first or most significant byte in the instruction, as shown below.

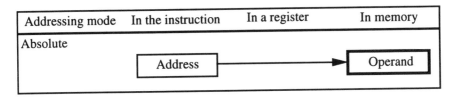

Addressing mode	In the instruction	In a register	In memory
Absolute	Address	→	Operand

Example

MOVE.B $1000,$2000

This instruction copies a byte from memory address 1000_{16} into memory address 2000_{16} using absolute addressing for both the source and destination operands. In RTL this is described by:

$$[M(\$2000)] \quad \leftarrow \quad [M(\$1000)]$$

There are two forms of absolute addressing, *absolute short* and *absolute long*, because the address can be held in the instruction using either 16 or 32 bits. When the short form is used, the 68000 sign extends the address to 32 bits before it is used to access the operand.

(4) Address register indirect addressing

With this form of addressing, the instruction specifies an address register, which points to the memory location containing the most significant byte of the operand, as illustrated below.

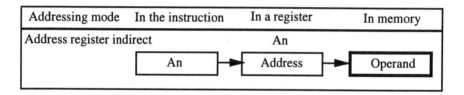

The syntax used to represent this addressing mode is (An). The brackets around An indicates that it is the 'content' of the address register which gives the actual or *effective address* of the operand.

Example
$$CLR.B \qquad (A2)$$

CLeaRs the byte whose memory address is held in register A2. In RTL this is described by:

$$[M([A2])] \quad \leftarrow \quad 0$$

(5) Address register indirect with post-increment addressing

This addressing mode is one of two variants on the last one except that **after** the operand has been accessed, the content of the address register is **incremented** by 1, 2 or 4, according to the size of the operand. This is illustrated below:

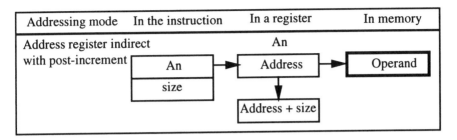

Addressing mode	In the instruction	In a register	In memory

The syntax used to represent this addressing mode is (An)+ where the 'plus sign' after the brackets is used to signify post-increment. The following examples illustrate how it works:

Example

MOVE.B (A0)+,D1

The byte contained in the memory location pointed to by A0 is copied into bits (0:7) of D1. Because a byte sized operand is used, the content of A0 is incremented by 1.

$$[D1(0:7)] \quad \leftarrow \quad [M([A0])]$$
$$[A0] \quad \leftarrow \quad [A0] + 1$$

Example

MOVE.W (A0)+,D2

The word contained in the memory location pointed to by A0 is copied into bits (0:15) of D2. Because a word sized operand is used, the content of A0 is incremented by 2.

$$[D2(0:15)] \quad \leftarrow \quad [M([A0])]$$
$$[A0] \quad \leftarrow \quad [A0] + 2$$

TQ 5.4   Write down an RTL description of the instruction:

MOVE.L (A0)+,D3

---

(6) Address register indirect with pre-decrement addressing

This is a second variant on the address register indirect addressing mode, in which the address register is **decremented** by 1, 2 or 4 according to the size of the operand, **before** the operand is accessed, as illustrated below.

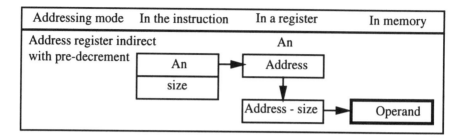

The syntax used to represent this addressing mode is – (An), where the 'minus sign' before the brackets is used to signify pre-decrement. The following examples illustrate how it works:

Example

$$\text{MOVE.B} - (A0), D1$$

Because a byte sized operand is specified, the content of A0 is decremented by 1. The byte contained in the memory location pointed to by A0 is then copied into bits (0:7) of D1.

$$[A0] \quad \leftarrow \quad [A0] - 1$$
$$[D1(0:7)] \quad \leftarrow \quad [M([A0])]$$

Example

$$\text{MOVE.L} - (A7), D1$$

Because a longword sized operand is specified, the content of A7 is decremented by 4. The byte contained in the memory location pointed to by A7 is then copied into bits (0:31) of D1.

$$[A7] \quad \leftarrow \quad [A7] - 4$$
$$[D1(0:31)] \quad \leftarrow \quad [M([A7])]$$

TQ 5.5   Write down an RTL description of the instruction:
           $\text{MOVE.W} - (A7), D3$

---

(7) *Program Counter relative with displacement addressing*

With this addressing mode, the effective address of the operand is found by adding a displacement, held in the operand field of the instruction, to the current value of the Program Counter, as shown below.

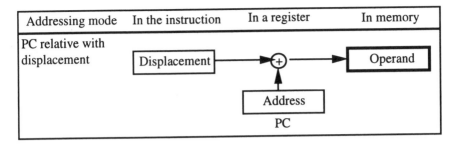

The syntax used for this addressing mode is (displacement, PC) or (symbol, PC).

Example

MOVE.W   (1000,PC), D1

Copy the word whose memory address is the sum of 1000 and the contents of the Program Counter, into D1.

$$[D1(0:15)] \quad \leftarrow \quad [M(1000+ [PC])]$$

(8) Address register indirect with displacement addressing

Instead of adding a displacement to the PC, to determine the effective address of the operand, the instruction can specify an address register to be used instead. This is illustrated below.

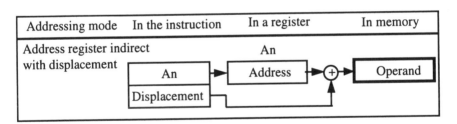

The syntax for this addressing mode is (displacement, An) or (symbol, An).

Example

MOVE.B   (100,A2),D0

Copy the byte at the memory address given by the sum of 100 and the contents of A2, into D0(0:7).

$$[D0(0:7)] \quad \leftarrow \quad [M(100 + [A2])]$$

5.4 Instruction Formats

Each 68000 instruction occupies between one and five words of memory. The first word is called the *operation word* and contains the opcode and the addressing modes to be used. The remaining words (if any) are used for data constants and/or absolute addresses. Figure 5.7 shows the general instruction format.

15	8 7	0
Operation Word		
Immediate operand (if any, 1 or 2 words)		
Source effective address (if any, 1 or 2 words)		
Destination effective address (if any, 1 or 2 words)		

Figure 5.7 General 68000 Instruction Format

The instruction coding scheme for the instructions MOVE, MOVEQ and BRA are illustrated in figure 5.8.

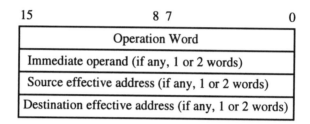

Figure 5.8 Operation word for the MOVE, MOVEQ and BRA

For a MOVE instruction, the 2-bit *size field* is (01 for a byte), (11 for a word) and (10 for a longword). The source and destination addressing modes are specified by 3 *mode bits* and 3 *register bits*. The mode field is coded according to the list given in table 5.1.

For a MOVEQ instruction, an 8-bit two's complement number is used for the immediate data field, which can represent integers in the range −128 to +127. A two's complement representation is also used for the displacement field of the BRA instruction, allowing forward and backward branching relative to the current value of the Program Counter. The displacement is 8 bits for the short form (suffix S) and 16 bits for the long form (suffix L). The long form requires an additional word to store the displacement.

Table 5.1 Coding of the mode field

Mode	Register	Description
000	register number	data register direct
001	register number	address register direct
111	100	immediate
111	001	absolute
010	register number	address register indirect
011	register number	address register indirect with post-increment
100	register number	address register indirect with pre-decrement
111	010	program counter relative
101	register number	address register indirect with displacement

Examples

	MOVE.B D1,D2
is coded as:	00 01 010 000 000 001 = 1401_{16}

	MOVE.W (A2)+,D7
is coded as:	00 11 111 000 011 010 = $3E1A_{16}$

	MOVEQ #3,D2
is coded as:	0111 010 0 00000011 = 7403_{16}

If the [PC] = 8002_{16} then: BRA.S $8008
  is coded as: 01100000 00000110 = 6006_{16}

TQ 5.6   How would MOVEQ # –1,D2 be coded?

TQ 5.7   If the [PC] = 8002_{16} then how would BRA $8000 be coded?

5.5 Assembly Code Examples

In this section we examine some simple 68000 assembly language programs. We begin by describing the layout of an assembly language program and the purpose of assembler directives.

(1) Assembler directives

Assembly language programs are normally written using a text editor and stored as a *source file*. The source file is then translated into an *object file* using an *assembler*. The object file contains machine code, which can be loaded into memory and executed on the target machine. An example of a simple assembly language program is given in table 5.2.

Table 5.2 Simple program to find the length of a string

label field	operation field	operand field	comment field
	ORG	$100	Origin for data
STRING	DC.B	'Hello World!'	String to be tested
	DC.B	$0D	Terminator
LEN	DS.B	1	One byte for length
CR	EQU	$0D	Carriage Return
	ORG	$200	Origin for program
START	LEA.L	STRING, A0	A0 points to STRING
	CLR.B	D0	Initialise counter
LOOP	CMPI.B	#CR, (A0)+	Check for end
	BEQ	DONE	If found then done
	ADDQ.B	#1, D0	Else increment count
	BRA.S	LOOP	Continue counting
DONE	MOVE.B	D0, LEN	Save count
	RTS		
	END		

The program is divided into four columns or *fields*: a *label* field; an *operation* field; an *operand* field; and a *comment* field.

The label field contains *symbolic names*, such as STRING, LEN, CR and LOOP to represent memory addresses or values. This relieves the programmer from having to know the actual memory addresses at which instructions are stored and makes the program more readable. For example, the instruction BRA.S   LOOP causes a backward branch to the instruction labelled LOOP. During assembly, the label LOOP is automatically replaced by the address of the instruction labelled LOOP, which is $206 for this program.

The comment field is optional and allows the programmer to clarify the purpose of a given instruction. Comments can also occupy a complete line if the first symbol on the line is a '*' or other special symbol recognised by the assembler. During the assembly process, all comments are ignored.

The operation and operand fields are used for instructions and assembler directives. Assembler directives are commands to the assembler itself and, with the exception of DC, do not cause any machine code to be generated. A summary of the five assembler directives common to most 68000 assemblers is given in table 5.3.

Table 5.3 Basic assembler directives

Assembler directive			Description
	ORG	*address*	The instructions and declarations following this directive are to be placed in memory beginning at address, *address*
[*label*]	DC.s	*n*	Initialise the contents of memory location, *label*, to *n*, where n has size, *s*, which can be byte (B) word (W) or Longword (L)
[*label*]	DS.s	*n*	Reserve storage space for *n* operands of size, *s*
sym	EQU	*value*	Equate the symbolic name, *sym*, to the value, *value*
	END		End of source program

* Note that [*label*] is optional

(2) Program examples

Program to find the length of a string

The program in table 5.2 is used to find the length of the string labelled, STRING and stores the result in memory at address, LEN. The string is terminated by the ASCII code for carriage return, $0D. Because the program begins with the assembler directive:

ORG $100

the label STRING refers to address $100.

The directives:

DC.B	'Hello World!'
DC.B	$0D
DS.B	1

then initialise the first few memory locations as shown below.

STRING =$100	'H'	'e'
$102	'l'	'l'
$104	'o'	'space'
$106	'W'	'o'
$108	'r'	'l'
$10A	'd'	'!'
$10C	$0D	**reserved**

* Note that 'H','e', etc are ASCII codes for the characters

The assembler directive:

CR   EQU $0D

equates the symbolic name CR, with the ASCII code $0D for carriage-return. This helps to make the program more readable.

TQ 5.8   What is the address represented by the label START?

Program execution begins with the first instruction:

LEA.L   STRING, A0

which loads the address STRING or $100, into address register A0.
The instruction:

CLR.B   D0

then sets bits (0:7) of D0 to 0, ready for counting the characters in the string.
The instruction:

CMPI.B   #CR, (A0)+

then compares the immediate data constant CR or $0D, with the ASCII code of the first character in the string 'H' or $48 (see Appendix A1). As they are clearly not the same, the Z-flag of the condition code register is cleared (Z = 0).

TQ 5.9   What will A0 contain after executing this instruction?

When the conditional branch instruction:

BEQ   DONE

is executed for the first time, a branch to the target address DONE, does **not** take place and control is passed to the next sequential instruction:

ADDQ.B   #1,D0

This adds 1 or increments register D0, which acts as a character counter. The next instruction:

BRA.S   LOOP

is an unconditional branch and forces program control back to the CMPI instruction at the address labelled LOOP. The instruction sequence is then repeated, each pass through the loop causing D0 to be incremented. Eventually A0 contains the address $10C, so that when CR is compared with (A0) or $0D, the Z-flag is set (Z = 1). This causes the instruction, BEQ DONE, to branch to its target address labelled DONE and cause execution of the instruction:

MOVE.B   D0,LEN

This instruction stores the character count that has accumulated in register D0, bits(0:7), into the reserved storage location LEN.

To terminate the program we have used a ReTurn from Subroutine (RTS) instruction. Depending upon the computer and operating system, this may or may not be an appropriate way to end assembly language programs. For example, you might use STOP or make a call to the operating system, with an instruction such as TRAP #11.

Program to find the factorial of a number

The assembly code fragment shown in table 5.4, determines the factorial of a number by referring to a look-up table labelled FTAB.

Using ORG directives, the program is divided into three sections: a data storage area for the table; an area for storing the subroutine; and an area for the MAIN or calling program. The subroutine FACT, which is terminated by an RTS instruction, finds the factorial of the number stored at address VALUE and puts the answer in the storage location RESULT.

Table 5.4 Program to find the factorial of a number

```
* Table of Factorial values
              ORG          $100
FTAB          DC.W         1              0! = 1
              DC.W         1              1! = 1
              DC.W         2              2! = 2
              DC.W         6              3! = 6
              DC.W         24             4! = 24
              DC.W         120            5! = 120
              DC.W         720            6! = 720
              DC.W         5040           7! = 5040
VALUE         DS.W         1
RESULT        DS.W         1

* Subroutine FACT, which finds factorial of number stored in VALUE
              ORG          $200
FACT          CLR.W        D0
              MOVE.W       VALUE, D0
              MULU         #2, D0
              MOVEA.W      D0, A0
              MOVE.W       (FTAB, A0), RESULT
              RTS

* Main program, which initialises VALUE and calls subroutine FACT
              ORG          $300
MAIN          MOVE.W       #5, VALUE
              BSR          FACT
              MOVE.W       RESULT, D0
              •
              •
              END
```

Before calling the subroutine, the main program must initialise the variable VALUE with the number whose factorial is to be found. Program execution begins in the main program with the instruction:

MOVE.W   #5, VALUE

which loads the number 5 into address VALUE. A branch is then made to the subroutine FACT, using a Branch to SubRoutine instruction:

BSR   FACT

This instruction uses the stack pointer register A7, to *push* the current value of the Program Counter (PC) onto the *stack*. The PC, which initially   points to the instruction (MOVE.W RESULT,D0), is then overwritten with the target address FACT. This is illustrated in figure 5.9, where the addresses of the MOVE.W instruction and FACT are $0000030A and $00000200 respectively.

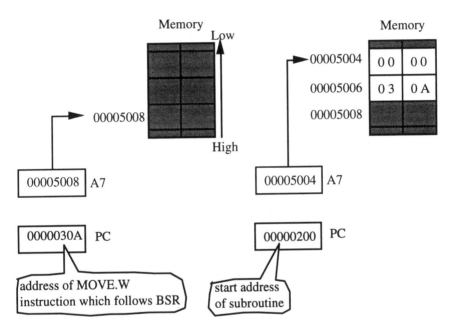

Figure 5.9 The stack during a subroutine call

Once the PC is loaded, the instructions:

        CLR.W   D0
        MOVE.W   VALUE,D0

are fetched and executed, causing the data register D0 bits(0:15) to be cleared and loaded with the contents of address VALUE, which is the number 5. The instructions:

        MULU   #2,D0
        MOVEA.W D0,A0

then multiply the number by 2 and move the result into address register A0.

In this program, A0 is used as a word index into the look-up table FTAB. The table is accessed using the next instruction:

MOVE.W   (FTAB,A0),RESULT

TQ 5.10   What will be the contents of memory address RESULT after executing
          this instruction?

The last instruction in the subroutine is RTS, which is a mnemonic for ReTurn from Subroutine. The action performed by this instruction can be represented in RTL as:

[PC]	$\leftarrow$	[M([A7])]	*pull* the return address from stack
[A7]	$\leftarrow$	[A7] + 4	then increment the stack pointer

This transfers control back to the main program, which continues with:

MOVE.W   RESULT,D0

This instruction saves the result provided by the subroutine call, in data register D0 bits (0:15).

Subroutines can be called several times during the execution of a program and can also be nested inside each other. Each time a subroutine is called, its return address is pushed onto the stack, causing the stack to 'grow' backwards towards low memory. As each subroutine call is completed, a return address is pulled from the stack, causing the stack to 'collapse'. The stack can also be used for passing parameters between a program and a subroutine or between one subroutine and another. This is done by pushing the parameters on to the stack before the subroutine is entered and pulling any results from the stack afterwards. The 68000 includes several powerful instructions to support stack manipulation.

5.6 Supervisor Mode

As we mentioned earlier, the 68000 can run in either user mode or supervisor mode. Supervisor mode is normally reserved for the monitor program or operating system, which is a mode in which all 68000 instructions can be executed. User mode is normally used for application programs and other system programs such as editors, compilers and assemblers. In user mode, certain *privileged instructions* cannot be executed and any attempt to do so raises an *exception*. Exceptions transfer control to the monitor or operating system (OS).

In addition to *privilege violation exceptions* there are other internally generated exceptions, such as TRAP #n instructions, which are used in user programs to call operating system functions. There are also externally generated exceptions caused by external circuits sending signals to the processor, such as interrupt signals. Interrupts are discussed in chapter 7.

5.7 Trace Mode

When the 68000 is running normally, the trace bit is clear (T = 0). If the trace bit is set (T = 1), by using the *privileged instruction*, MOVE to SR, then a *trace exception* is raised after **each** instruction is executed. When the exception is raised, control is passed to an *exception handler* or *interrupt service routine*, which can be arranged to display the contents of the processor registers. The trace mode therefore offers a useful facility for debugging programs.

5.8 Summary

1. The Motorola 68000 has the following registers:

   - Eight 32-bit data registers, which support Byte(B), Word(W) and Longword(L) operations.

   - Eight 32-bit address registers, which act as pointer registers when accessing data structures such as tables. A0 to A6 are for general use while A7 is used as dedicated stack pointer. Address registers support W and L operations. Sign extension is used when moving a word into an address register.

   - A 16-bit Status Register, the lower user byte is a condition code register and the upper system byte is used for the interrupt mask, trace bit and supervisor bit.

   - A 32-bit Program Counter register, which points to the next instruction to be executed.

2. The Motorola 68000 instructions can be divided up into the following classes:

   - Data Movement   • Program Control   • Others
   - Arithmetic and Logic   • Bit manipulation

3. The Motorola 68000 supports a large number of addressing modes including:

   - Data Register Direct   Dn
   - Address Register Direct   An
   - Address Register Indirect   (An)
   - Address Register Indirect with pre-decrement   – (An)
   - Address Register Indirect with post-increment   (An) +
   - Program Counter relative with displacement   (disp, PC)
   - Address Register indirect with displacement   (disp, An)

4. The Motorola 68000 uses a number of different instruction formats which occupy between one and five words of memory. The first or operation word contains the opcode and specifies the addressing modes to be used.

5. Assembly language programs are divided up into four fields:

   - an optional label field
   - an operation field which contains instruction mnemonics and assembler directives
   - an operand field for addressing modes or information associated with any assembler directives
   - an optional comment field

   Assembler directives usually include as a minimum, the directives:
   ORG, DC, DS, EQU and END.

5.9 Answers to Text Questions

TQ 5.1 $[D1(0:31)]$ $\leftarrow [M(0)]$

TQ 5.2   Because of suffix B, this instruction reads bits (0:7) of data register D0 (source) and copies them into memory location 000006_{16} (destination).

TQ 5.3 $8FFF_{16}$ is $1000\ 1111\ 1111\ 1111_2$ with a sign bit $= 1$.
The 68000 therefore sign extends this 1 into bits (16:31) by storing $FFFF8FFF_{16}$.

TQ 5.4 $[D3(0:31)]$ $\leftarrow [M([A0])]$
$[A0]$ $\leftarrow [A0] + 4$

TQ 5.5 $[A7]$ $\leftarrow [A7] - 2$
$[D3(0:15)]$ $\leftarrow$ $[M([A7])]$

TQ 5.6   Using 8-bit two's complement representation, $-1 = FF$. Therefore the instruction would be coded as $74FF_{16}$

TQ 5.7   To branch to address \$8000, then the displacement $= -2$, which is FE_{16} in 8-bit two's complement representation. The instruction would therefore be coded as $60FE_{16}$

TQ 5.8   Because of the ORG \$200 directive which precedes it, START represents the address \$200.

TQ 5.9   A0 will be incremented by 1, because this is a byte sized operation. It will therefore contain the address \$101.

TQ 5.10 $[RESULT] = 120_{10}$

5.10 Exercises

1. Write down the machine code representation of the following instructions.

    a) MOVE.W D7,D3 b) MOVEQ #5,D6

2. In RTL, the effect calling a subroutine, BSR TEST, is given by:

$$[A7] \quad\quad \leftarrow \quad\quad [A7] - 4$$
$$[M([A7])] \quad\quad \leftarrow \quad\quad [PC]$$
$$[PC] \quad\quad \leftarrow \quad\quad [PC] + d$$

    where d is the 8-bit or 16-bit two's complement displacement to the address
    labelled, TEST.
    Give a precise description of each statement, and write down a pair of similar
    RTL statements for the effects caused by an RTS instruction.

3. Write suitable instructions to perform the following English statements.

    a) Exchange the lower and upper words of register D0 and then move the
        contents of D0(0:7) into memory location 400500_{16}

    b) Move the literal, 5, into data register D3 and then increment it by 1.

    c) Add the byte contained in the memory address pointed to by A1, to bits (0:7)
        of D0. Then add the word contained in the next pair of consecutive memory
        addresses, to bits (0:15) of D1.

    d) Test bit 4 of data register D2 and if it is zero, branch to the subroutine
        labelled ZERO. Otherwise branch to the address labelled LOOP.

4. Why would the following program fragment raise an address error exception?

```
                ORG       $100
VALUE           DS.B      1
                MOVE.B    #$FF,VALUE
```

5.   For the program segment listed below

	ORG	$100
CODE	DC.B	$30
	DC.W	$3132
	DC.L	$33343536
VALUE	DS.B	1
DIGIT	EQU	4
	ORG	$200
MAIN	LEA	CODE, A0
	MOVE.B	(DIGIT, A0), VALUE
	RTS	
	END	

a) What are the addresses represented by the labels, CODE, DIGIT, VALUE and MAIN?

b) What will be the contents of address, VALUE, immediately after calling the subroutine MAIN?

References

Clements, A (1994), *68000 Family Assembly Language*, PWS International Thomson Pub Co, London

Stenstrom, P (1992), *68000 Microcomputer Organization and Programming*, Prentice Hall Ltd, New Jersey.

6 Computer Memory

The memory system of a general purpose computer is implemented using a number of different storage components. The purpose of this chapter is to describe the organisation of these components and the technologies used to implement them.

6.1 Memory Hierarchy

A memory hierarchy has more than one level of storage, each level having a different speed and size. The technologies used to implement the memory components at each level include fast semiconductor technology for the internal components close to the CPU and slower magnetic and optical surface technologies for the external components that are further away. Figure 6.1 illustrates a typical memory hierarchy.

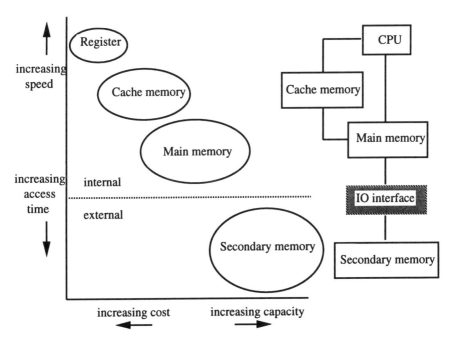

Figure 6.1 A memory hierarchy

Processor memory, implemented as a set of high-speed registers, occupies the highest level in the hierarchy. The register set only provides a very limited storage capacity and, as we found in chapter 5, serves only as a temporary storage area for instructions and operands.

Main memory provides the largest internal storage area that can be directly accessed by the CPU, having a typical storage capacity of between about 1 and 8 Mbytes. To reduce cost, main memory is normally implemented using Dynamic Random Access Memory (DRAM) chips. Because DRAM operates at around one tenth of the speed of the CPU logic, it tends to act as a bottleneck, reducing the rate at which the processor can fetch and execute instructions. To compensate for this, many systems include a small high-speed cache memory.

Cache memory sits between the CPU and main memory and is usually implemented using more expensive Static Random Access Memory (SRAM) technology. This transparent memory is used for storing frequently used program segments. Each time the CPU requests an instruction or data word, the cache is always checked first. If the information is found in the cache, a 'hit' occurs and the instruction or data word is rapidly retrieved and passed directly to the processor. If the information is not in the cache, a 'miss' takes place and the slower main memory is accessed instead.

Memory which is not directly accessible by the CPU is called external memory and includes secondary storage devices such as magnetic disks, tapes and optical storage devices, such as CD-ROMs. These devices, which must be accessed through input-output (IO) interface circuits, are the slowest components in the memory hierarchy. They provide a high-capacity storage area for programs and data not immediately required by the processor.

TQ 6.1   Contrast the cost, in pence per bit, of storing information in primary and secondary memory, given the following data:

1 Mbyte of DRAM costs £20 and a 200 Mbyte hard disk costs £100.

A memory hierarchy is therefore used because slow speed memory is cheaper than high speed memory and because only currently executing program segments need to be held in internal memory.

6.2 Semiconductor Technology

Integrated circuits (ICs), such as microprocessors and memory chips, are fabricated from a class of materials called *semiconductors*. This name arises because these materials can conduct electricity better than *insulators*, which normally do not conduct electricity, but not as well as *metals*, which are good electrical conductors. Metals are good conductors because they have a large number of 'free' negatively charged *electrons* to carry the electrical current through the material. Insulators on the other hand, have virtually no free electrons, all electrons being 'tightly' bound to their parent atoms. Currently the most widely used form of semiconducting material is *silicon*.

Figure 6.2(a) illustrates the electronic structure of a silicon atom. The atom has a total of fourteen negatively charged electrons that are bound to its positively charged nucleus through electrostatic attraction.

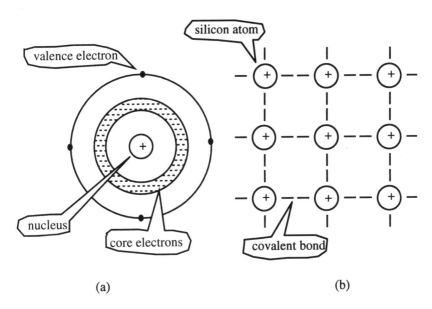

(a)   (b)

Figure 6.2 (a) Silicon atom (b) Silicon crystal

The four outermost electrons are called *valence electrons* while the ten innermost electrons are called *core electrons*. When silicon atoms are joined together in a crystal, as shown in figure 6.2(b), the 'loosely' bound valence electrons are shared with neighbouring atoms and form *covalent bonds*. These bonds hold the silicon atoms together at fixed sites in the crystal and give the crystal its regular lattice structure.

Because the crystal lattice is constantly vibrating, pairs of atoms sometimes move far enough apart to break bonds and free some of the valence electrons. These free electrons can then wander through the crystal and are available for carrying electric current. Electric current is also carried by the movement of *holes*, which are formed when core electrons break loose. The movement of these holes is illustrated in figure 6.3.

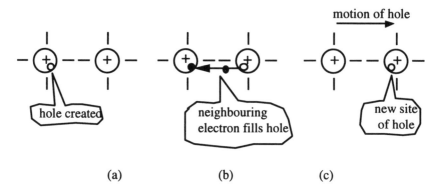

Figure 6.3 Movement of holes in a semiconductor

Once a hole has been created, as shown in figure 6.3(a), a bound core electron from an adjacent atom can break loose and fill the hole, as shown in figure 6.3(b). To fill the hole, the electron leaves behind a new hole in the core of its parent atom. This effectively causes the original hole to move to the site vacated by the electron, as shown in figure 6.3(c). Because holes move in the opposite direction to electrons, they behave as though they carry a positive charge.

Although pure semiconductors have holes and electrons to carry current, there are too few of them for this current to be useful. However, by *doping* the semiconductor with traces of impurity, it is possible to increase the number of holes or electrons and hence the *electrical conductivity*. When a semiconductor is doped to enhance the number of electrons, it is called *n-type* and when it is doped to enhance the number of holes, it is called *p-type*. By selectively doping different areas of a silicon wafer, IC manufacturers can construct *transistors*, *resistors* and *capacitors* and interconnect them to form useful circuits. The most widely used ICs fall into two main categories: bipolar and metal-oxide semiconductor (MOS) devices.

Bipolar devices use both holes and electrons to carry current. The basic building block of these devices is the *bipolar transistor*, shown in figure 6.4. In digital circuits, bipolar transistor operate as current controlled switches.

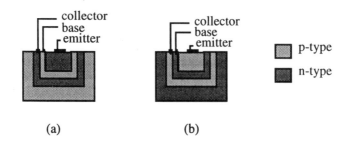

Figure 6.4 (a) npn and (b) pnp bipolar transistors

When suitable bias voltages are applied to its terminals, a small current injected into the *base* of the transistor, turns it on and causes a large current to flow between its *collector* and *emitter*. In this state, the emitter is electrically connected to the collector and the switch is closed. The switch is opened by removing the base current and stopping the current flow, which electrically isolates the collector from the emitter.

MOS devices use *unipolar* or *Field-Effect Transistors* (FETs). A FET can use either holes or electrons to carry current, an n-channel MOSFET (NMOS) using electrons and a p-channel MOSFET (PMOS) using holes. For the NMOS transistor shown in figure 6.5, the source and drain terminals are connected to two n-type regions of semiconductor that are formed in a p-type substrate, while the gate terminal is insulated from the substrate by a thin oxide layer.

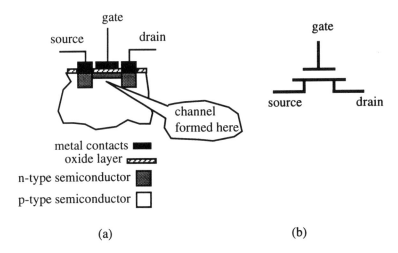

Figure 6.5 (a) NMOS Field-Effect Transistor (b) Circuit symbol

When a positive voltage is applied to the *gate*, an n-type channel is formed under the oxide layer, which provides a current path between the source and drain terminals and turns the transistor on. As with bipolar transistor, this electrically connects these terminals together and effectively closes the switch. The switch is opened by removing the gate voltage, which causes the channel to disappear and stops further current flow. A MOSFET therefore acts as a voltage controlled switch.

Because NMOS and its offspring, high-speed MOS (HMOS) are both faster than PMOS, devices built from PMOS transistors are seldom used. However, a popular form of low-power MOS technology in widespread use is Complementary MOS (CMOS), which uses both PMOS and NMOS transistors.

6.3 Semiconductor Memory Chips

The basic element of a memory chip is the *memory cell*, which can store a single binary digit. These cells are often grouped together to form words, each cell in the group sharing a common address. RAM cells can be read and written to, while ROM cells are either read only or in the case of programmable ROMs, read mostly. We begin this section by looking at semiconductor RAM.

(1) Random Access Memory (RAM)

There are two basic types of semiconductor RAM: Static-RAM (SRAM) and Dynamic-RAM (DRAM). The internal organisation of a typical SRAM memory chip is shown in figure 6.6.

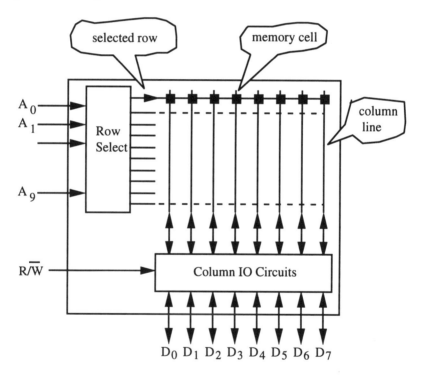

Figure 6.6 1024 × 8 bit Static RAM chip organisation

The cells are arranged in a matrix with rows and columns. An address supplied on the address lines A0,..,A9 is used to select a particular row, each cell in the row being connected to a separate column line. The cells are arranged in 8's, which we call *byte organised*. The column lines are used to transfer data bytes between the addressed row and the data lines D0,..,D7 which connect the chip to the data bus.

TQ 6.2 How many rows can the ten address lines A0,..,A9 select?

Reading and writing data is controlled by the 'read-write' ($R/\overline{W}$) control line, which is connected to the column IO circuit. A read operation is selected by taking this line high and a write operation is selected by taking the line low. This latter state is indicated by a bar over the W.

SRAM cells store data using cross-coupled transistor circuits acting as R-S flip-flops (see §2.3). Because bipolar or MOS versions of these cells require four or six transistors per cell, SRAM chips can store fewer bits per mm^2 of silicon than DRAM. They are also more expensive in terms of the cost/bit of storage space. The main advantage of SRAM over DRAM is its shorter access time (see table 6.1). A typical SRAM chip is shown in figure 6.7.

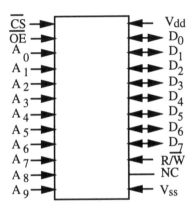

Figure 6.7 1024 × 8 bit SRAM chip

The chip select pin, $\overline{CS}$, is used to select the chip for read or write access and the output enable pin, $\overline{OE}$, is used during a read operation, to gate data from the memory array to the output data pins $D_0,..,D_7$. The pins labelled V_{dd} and V_{ss} are for supplying power to the chip.

TQ 6.3   What does the bar over the chip select pin indicate?

DRAMs store information using one transistor per memory cell and currently provide the most compact and low-cost form of semiconductor memory. Each storage element is basically a capacitor (a device for storing charge), with a MOS transistor being used to enable reading and writing. A DRAM cell is illustrated in figure 6.8.

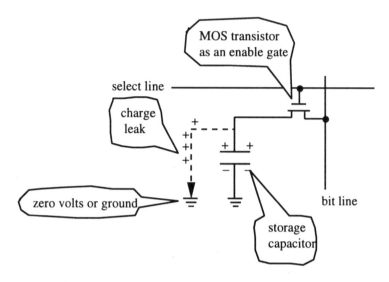

Figure 6.8 DRAM memory cell

To store a '1' or '0' in the cell, the select line is first taken high, which turns the MOS transistor (enable gate) **on** and connects the bit line to the capacitor. If the bit line is then taken high, a charge is transferred on to the capacitor and a '1' is stored and if it is taken low, any charge already on the capacitor is removed and a '0' is stored. After removing the voltage from the select line, the enable gate is turned **off** and the storage cell is isolated from the bit line. When a '1' is stored, the charge on the capacitor immediately begins to leak away, as indicated in the diagram. To maintain the charge, a special *refresh circuit* is used, which periodically renews the charge on all cells about once every 16 ms.

Reading is performed by simultaneously taking both the select and bit lines high. Using current sensing circuitry, the amount of charge transferred on to the cell is used to determine whether a '1' or a '0' is stored. Because this operation is destructive and alters the charge state of the cell, the sense circuit is responsible for restoring this state immediately after a read operation, either by adding charge or by removing it. This causes a time delay between successive requests to read a DRAM cell, which we call the *cycle time*.

DRAM cells are usually organised into a square matrix, with separate decoders for the rows and columns, as shown in figure 6.9.

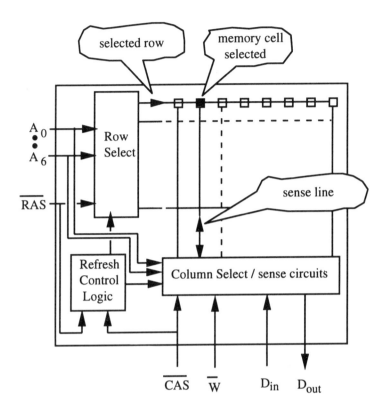

Figure 6.9 16384 × 1 bit DRAM organisation

To read a particular cell, the row address is provided on $A_0,..,A_6$ and latched into the row select decoder by a *row-address strobe* ($\overline{RAS}$). This is followed by the column address, which is latched into the column select decoder by a *column-address strobe* ($\overline{CAS}$). After a short time delay, the data bit appears at D_{out}.

Data is written into a selected cell by applying the data bit to D_{in} and by asserting the write control signal, $\overline{W}$, just before the column address is latched with the $\overline{CAS}$ strobe. Periodic refreshing is then carried out using an internal address generator and an external timing circuit. The timing circuit applies pulses to the address generator using the $\overline{RAS}$ and $\overline{CAS}$ strobes, which refreshes the memory chip a row at a time.

Figure 6.10 shows a typical *bit organised* DRAM chip. Because each chip only stores one bit, an 8-bit word, for example, would be stored using eight chips. A popular way of providing this form of memory is with *Single In-line Memory Modules* (SIMMs). These modules combine several chips on a small circuit board that is plugged into a retaining socket on the main memory board.

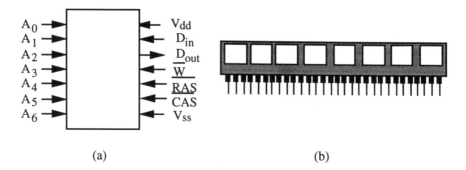

(a)   (b)

Figure 6.10 (a) 16384 × 1bit DRAM chip (b) 8-bit SIMM

(2) Read Only Memory (ROM)

ROMs are normally used for programs and data tables that must be immediately resident within the machine when power is first applied. ROMs fall into two classes: fixed and programmable.

Fixed or *Mask-programmable ROMs* have bit patterns which are set into the chips memory matrix during manufacture. Using an appropriate photographic mask, transistors are created at selected junctions between row and column lines, as shown in figure 6.11.

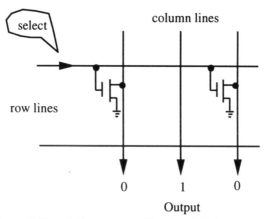

Figure 6.11 ROM memory cells using MOS transistors

In use, the column lines are normally held high, so that when a row is selected by taking the select line high, those transistors connected to columns are switched on. Because the drains of these transistors are now electrically connected to their sources, which are at zero volts, the selected columns are pulled to zero volts, producing a pattern of 1s and 0s at the output. Mask-programmable ROMs are expensive to produce in small quantities and are therefore only used for large scale production.

Programmable ROMs (PROMs), normally refer to a bipolar read only memory in which memory cells contain *fusible links* between the row and column lines. These links can be broken or 'blown' by passing a suitable current through selected cells, to form the required bit patterns. Because the fused-links cannot be restored, PROMs can only be programmed once.

Erasable Programmable ROMs (EPROMs) can be programmed, erased and then reprogrammed several times. For this reason EPROMs are sometimes referred to as *read mostly* memory. A popular form of EPROM is the *ultraviolet erasable ROM*, which uses special floating gate MOS transistors for storing the bit patterns. The transistors behave in a similar way to the fused links, except that they are normally open and are closed by injecting charge on to their gates from a high-voltage supply. Their advantage over PROMs is that they can be restored to their open state by exposing the cells to ultraviolet light through a small window in the top of the chip. This normally takes about 20 minutes. An EPROM, organised as $16K \times 8$-bit, is illustrated in figure 6.12.

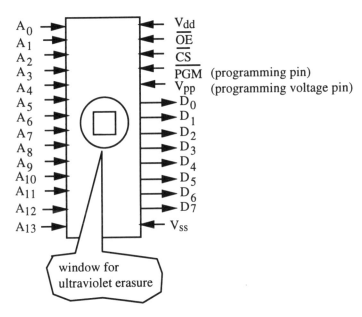

Figure 6.12 $16K \times 8$-bit ultraviolet EPROM

Electrically Erasable Programmable ROMs (EEPROMs) are like UV-erasable EPROMs except that they can be programmed and erased electrically, which allows them to be updated in situ. They are more flexible than EPROMs and allow individual bytes to be addressed and altered separately. Unfortunately, write operations take thousands of times longer than read operations.

(3) Semiconductor device characteristics

Table 6.1 summarises the main characteristics associated with the semiconductor memory devices we have discussed in this section.

Table 6.1 Typical semiconductor device characteristics (1995)

Memory Type	Technology	Alterability	Permanence	Access Time/ns
SRAM	bipolar	read/write	volatile	~ 25
DRAM	MOS	read/write	volatile	~ 50

Memory Type	Write Mechanism	Alterability	Erasure Mechanism	Access Time/ns
PROM	fused links	read only	none	~ 25
EPROM	electrical	read mostly	UV light (chip level)	~120
EEPROM	electrical	read mostly	electrical (byte level)	~120

The *access time*, is the average time required to read a word from memory and deliver it to its output terminals.

For SRAM, there is no difference between the access time and the *cycle time*, or minimum time between memory requests. This is not so for DRAM, which due to the destructive nature of read operations and the need to periodically refresh the charge stored on cells, has a cycle time which is greater than its access time. With each new generation of DRAM, semiconductor manufacturers have managed to reduce both the cycle time and the access time, as shown in figure 6.13. Current DRAMs have access times of about 50 ns and cycle times of about 90 ns.

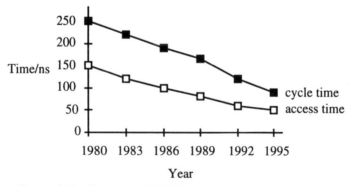

Figure 6.13 Changes in DRAM performance with generation

When connecting SRAM or DRAM chips to the system bus, these timing constraints need to be taken into consideration.

6.4 Processor-Memory Bus

(1) Address decoding

A computer memory system usually contains several RAM and ROM chips connected to the processor by a system bus, as shown in figure 6.11. Reading or writing to memory is carried out by using the lower order address lines to select a location within a chip and the upper address lines to select the chip itself, through the chips select pin, $\overline{CS}$. Only when selected, is a chip electrically connected to the data bus.

In figure 6.14 the lower fourteen address lines A0-A13 are used to select one of the 16K locations within a chip, and the two upper address lines A14,A15 are decoded to select one of the four chips. You will notice that the R/$\overline{W}$ control line is only connected to the RAM chips, as the ROMs can only be read when selected.

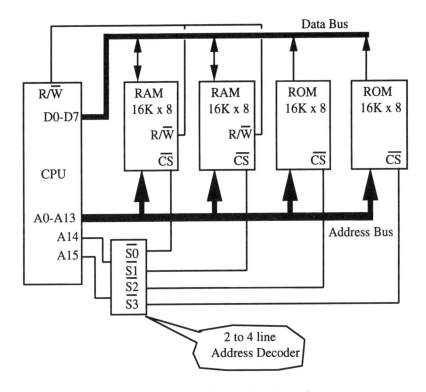

Figure 6.14 Simple address decoding scheme

Worked Example

A truth-table for the 2-to-4 line decoder (see §2.2), is given below

A15	A14	S0	S1	S2	S3
0	0	0	1	1	1
0	1	1	0	1	1
1	0	1	1	0	1
1	**1**	**1**	**1**	**1**	**0**

Which chip would be selected by the address, $C000_{16}$?

Solution

$C000_{16}$ = 1100 0000 0000 0000_2. With both A15 and A14 high, the decoder would cause the output S3 to go low and activate the ROM chip on the far right of figure 6.14.

By decoding the upper address lines in this way, the 2^{16} (64K) memory address space, accessible by the CPU, is mapped into **four** 16K regions, as shown in figure 6.15.

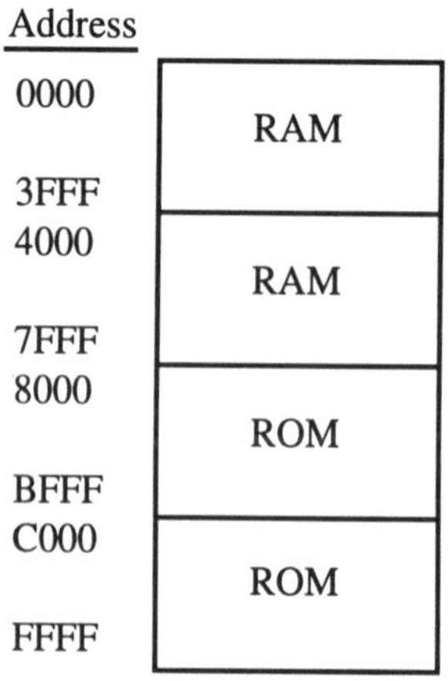

Figure 6.15 Memory-map corresponding to figure 6.14

In addition to RAM and ROM chips, interface chips that control IO operations, can also form part of the main-memory address space. Memory-mapped IO is discussed in the chapter 7.

(2) Bus timing

To co-ordinate the transfer of data between the processor and memory, some form of timing must be used. With a *synchronous bus*, a master clock provides the timing reference source, which can be read by all devices connected to the bus. The clock transmits a regular sequence of 1s and 0s, called *clock cycles*. A timing diagram specifies when various bus events should take place relative to this clock.

For the simplified SRAM timing diagram shown in figure 6.16, a read or write operation begins when the clock makes a '1' to '0' transition. Shortly after this transition, the CPU puts an address on the address bus, the address bus being represented by two parallel lines, which are crossed at those instants when the address changes.

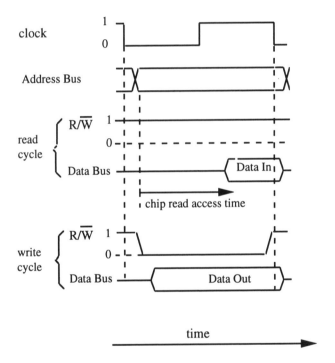

Figure 6.16 Timing diagram for a synchronous bus

During a read cycle, the R/W̄ line is held at logic 1 and data is read from the data bus into the CPU, towards the end of the clock cycle. Before the CPU reads this data, the memory chip must provide stable data on the bus.

During a write cycle, the CPU puts data on to the data bus and signals a write operation by taking the R/W̄ line low. Towards the end of the cycle, the CPU restores the R/W̄ line to logic 1, latching the data into the memory chip.

TQ 6.4   Given the following timing data, what is the largest acceptable read
          access time for the memory chips connected to this bus?
          • clock cycle time = 500 ns
          • valid address occurs 200 ns after start of bus cycle
          • data read from bus 50 ns before end of bus cycle

When there are memory chips with different access times, the clock must be selected to allow the slowest component to participate in data transfer. Each read or write operation is then completed in a time called the *memory cycle* time, which in our example, is the time for one clock cycle.

DRAM timing is more complicated than SRAM timing, because of the way in which the row and column addresses are set up and because the cycle time is longer than the access time.

6.5 Cache Memory

As we mentioned earlier, a semiconductor cache memory is a small (to reduce cost) high-speed memory that acts as a buffer between the CPU and main memory. The cache alleviates the bottleneck caused by the difference in speed between the CPU and main memory, by taking advantage of a property of program behaviour called the *principle of locality*.

(1) Principle of locality

Because of the nature of programs and the way data is structured, it is found that during execution, memory references do not take place randomly, but are localised. For example, programs tend to reuse data and instructions that have recently been used (*temporal locality*) and instructions and data referenced close together in time, also tend to also be close together in memory (*spatial locality*). We can appreciate how this locality arises by referring back to the simple program to find the length of a string, which we discussed in the last chapter (see §5.5).

This program used a loop to count the number of characters in a string. When the loop was entered, the instructions forming the body of the loop were reused over and over again until the terminating byte was reached. While this portion of the program was being executed, memory references were clustered into two regions: one just above address $200, where the loop instructions were stored and the other near address $100, where the characters were stored.

Cache memory systems exploit this general property of program behaviour and enhance system performance by maintaining the currently active portions of a program in the high-speed cache. How these regions are identified will now be discussed.

(2) Principle of cache operation

A semiconductor cache contains a limited number of *slots* or *lines* for storing *blocks* of main memory. Each block is typically four to sixteen words. During program execution, instead of reading instructions or data words directly from main memory, the CPU first searches for them in the cache. If the word is found, a 'hit' is signalled and the word is transferred from the cache to the CPU, as shown in figure 6.17(a).

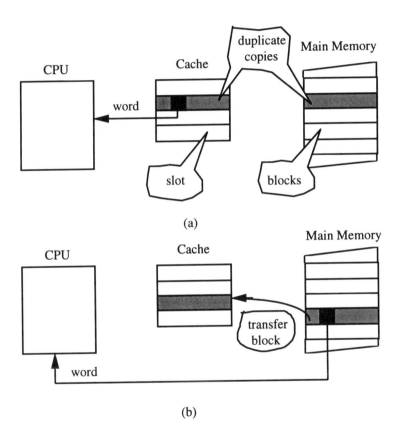

(a)

(b)

Figure 6.17 (a) A cache 'hit' (b) A cache 'miss'

If the word is missing from the cache, it is fetched from main memory, the cache being updated with the *block* containing the word, as shown in figure 6.17(b). Because of spatial locality, this increases the probability of finding, at least in the short term, subsequent words in the cache.

A measure of cache performance is the *hit-ratio* (h), which is the fraction of all memory references that are satisfied by the cache and which avoid the need to access main memory. If the access time for the cache and main memory are t_c and t_m respectively, then the average time t_{av} to access a word, is given by:

$$t_{av} = ht_c + (1 - h)t_m$$

Notice that if all memory references are in the cache, (h = 1), the average access time is reduced to that of the cache, while if there is no cache present, (h=0), then the access time is equal to that of main memory.

TQ 6.5   If t_c = 20 ns, t_m = 80 ns and h = 0.9, then by how much is the system speeded up by using this cache memory?

A cache memory must be organised in such a way as to allow fast and efficient word searching. To do this, blocks of memory must be mapped into cache locations using some form of mapping function. We will now consider how this can be done.

(3) Associative cache

With an associative cache, blocks of main memory are mapped into cache slots and marked with a block number or *tag*, as shown in figure 6.18(a). The tag is determined by the upper portion of the memory address, called the *tag field*, which in this example is the upper 20-bits of the 24-bit address. The lower 4 bits or *word field* determines the position of a byte within the block.

During a cache search, the tag field of the address generated by the CPU is simultaneously compared with the tags stored in the cache, as shown in figure 6.18(b). If the tag field matches a tag in the cache, a 'hit' occurs and the byte selected by the word field is transferred to the CPU. If a 'miss' occurs, the byte is fetched from main memory and the 16-byte memory block containing the requested byte is inserted into a spare cache slot. This data transfer adds to the time penalty of a cache miss.

Parallel searching is carried out using special electronic circuits built into the cache. These circuits are complex and add to its cost. To reduce this cost, alternative cache organisations are often used, which employ ordinary random access memory.

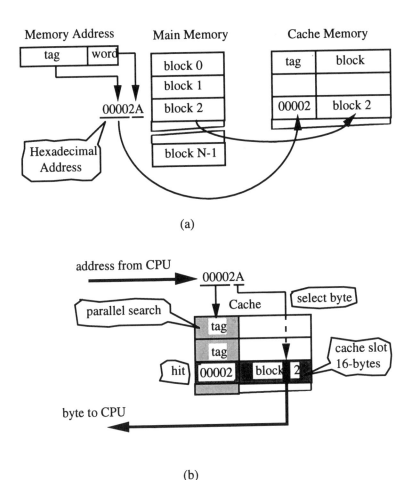

Figure 6.18 (a) Associative cache organisation (b) A cache search

---

TQ 6.6   How would the byte 7A at address $FE0802_{16}$ be stored in the cache?

---

(4) Direct-mapped cache

With a directly mapped cache organisation, the problem of searching the cache is avoided by assigning each memory block to just one cache slot. The slot number of a block can be derived from its memory address, allowing the block to be retrieved from the cache by simply indexing into it.

Figure 6.19 illustrates how this mapping scheme works for a cache having 4096 slots and 16 bytes per slot.

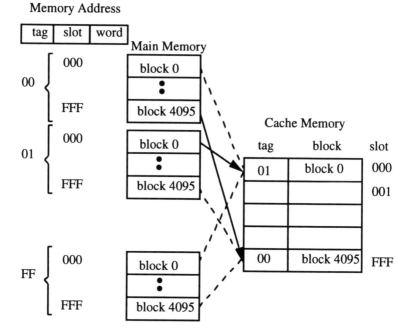

Figure 6.19 Direct-mapped cache

The 24-bit memory address is divided up into three fields: a tag field, a slot field and a word field. The 8-bit tag field divides main memory into 256 groups of blocks, each block being assigned a slot number given by the 12-bit slot field. Although no more than one block from the same set can occupy a given cache slot, blocks from different sets can. To identify the group to which a block belongs, its tag must be stored along with it.

When accessing the cache, as shown in figure 6.20, the slot field of the address generated by the CPU is used to index the cache. The stored tag is then compared with the tag field of the CPU address. If they match, a 'hit' occurs and the word field is used to select the appropriate byte, which is then passed to the CPU.

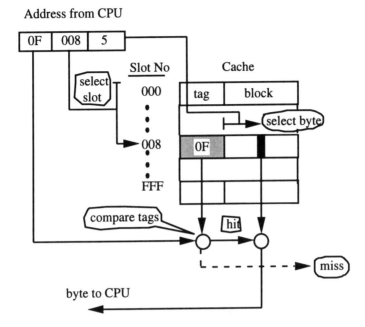

Figure 6.20 Accessing a direct-mapped cache

If a 'miss' occurs, the full CPU address is used to fetch the byte from main memory and the cache line is filled with the block containing the byte.

TQ 6.7   Into which main memory locations would a block stored in slot OFF and having a tag 5A be moved, if the block had to be swapped out of the cache to make room for another?

The main problem with direct mapping is that blocks **share** specific cache slots and only one of these blocks can be in the cache at any one time. If a program frequently accesses two blocks that map into the same slot, then blocks must repeatedly be swapped in and out of the cache, severely degrading its performance. One solution to this problem is to organise the cache so that more than one block can occupy the same slot. This is called set-associative mapping.

(5) Set-associative cache

A set associative cache can store a number of tag-block pairs in each cache line, the number of pairs forming a set. A two-way cache organisation, is shown in figure 6.21.

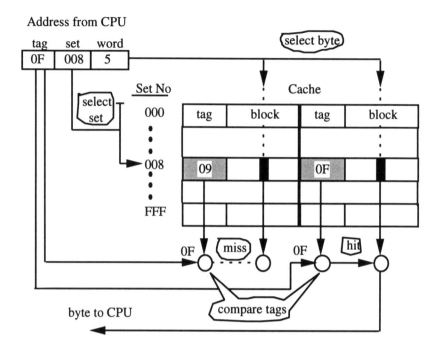

Figure 6.21 Two-way set-associative cache organisation

Each main memory block is mapped into one of the 2^{12} sets according to the set-field of its 24-bit memory address. Thus the 16-byte block between 09<u>008</u>0 and 09008F maps into set 8, as does the block between 0F<u>008</u>0 and 0F<u>008</u>F, each block occupying a separate slot and being identified by a unique tag.

When the cache is accessed by the CPU, the set-field is used as an index into the cache in the same way as the slot field was used with the direct-mapping scheme. Having identified the set, both tags are compared simultaneously with the tag-field of the address. If a 'hit' occurs, the byte selected by the word field is passed to the CPU, otherwise the byte is fetched from main memory and a new block is transferred into the set.

When a 'miss' occurs and the set is full, it becomes necessary to replace one of the tag-block entries in the set with a new tag-block pair. A popular form of *replacement algorithm* is the *least recently used* (LRU), which as its name suggests, replaces the block that has been least recently accessed by the CPU. To determine which block this applies to, an extra bit is included with each cache entry, which is modified each time the CPU accesses that set. Another replacement policy is *first-in-first-out* (FIFO), which replaces the block that has been in the set the longest.

(6) Cache coherency

An important issue of cache design is how to deal with writes. If the cache is only used for storing instructions (*instruction cache*), then this is not a problem because instructions are only read. If on the other hand, the cache is used for storing data (*data cache*) or data and instruction (*unified cache*), then reading, modifying and writing data back into the cache can create a situation where the data stored in the cache is inconsistent with that in main memory. To maintain data consistency or *cache coherency*, some form of *write policy* must be adopted.

One of the simplest policies to implement is *write-through*, which maintains consistency by following any cache write operations with a write to main memory. One disadvantage in doing this, is that the CPU has to wait for the write operation to complete and this can severely degrade performance when there are multiple writes to the same block.

An alternative and widely used policy is *write-back*, where instead of immediately writing the block back to main memory, a status bit is used to mark the cache line as modified or *dirty*. Only when it becomes necessary to replace the modified block, is it copied back to main memory. This allows the CPU to write and read at the same speed and reduces the wait or *stall time*. Unfortunately, if there are special input/output controllers in the system, that can move data to/from main memory without the intervention of the CPU, such as DMA controllers (see §7.5), then maintaining consistency in this way can be a problem.

6.6 Secondary Memory

The two main technologies used for secondary storage devices are magnetic surface and optical technology.

(1) Magnetic surface technology

Dynamic magnetic storage systems record data by inducing dipoles on to a moving magnetic surface. To read or write data, the surface is moved past a read/write head, as shown in figure 6.22(a).

Data is written on to the surface by driving a current through the head coil windings. The direction of the current determines the orientation of the dipole and hence whether a binary '1' or '0' is stored. With *horizontal recording*, the dipoles lie along the direction of motion of the surface, whilst with *vertical recording*, they are oriented in perpendicular direction. During a read operation, the surface flux generated by the dipoles (figure 6.22(b)) induces a voltage signal across the coil, the polarity being dependent upon the direction of the flux lines. The size of this signal depends upon the linear velocity of the surface and the number of turns in the coil. After passing through the sense amplifier, this signal is processed and the encoded data extracted.

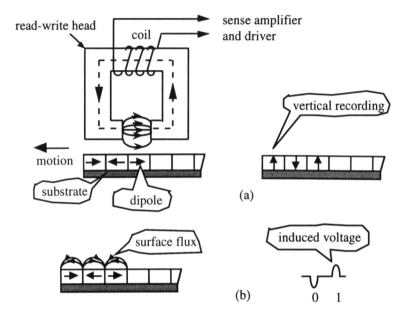

Figure 6.22 Magnetic surface recording

(2) *Magnetic disk storage*

A widely used form of secondary storage is the *hard disk*, shown in figure 6.23(a). Data is magnetically recorded on to circular *tracks* using a small read-write head, which floats about 2.5 micron[1] above the surface of the rotating disk. The head is attached to an actuator arm, which allows it to be stepped radially across the surface from one track to another. Tracks are divided up into *sectors*, each sector being used to store a block of data.

With a *multiple-disk* system, as shown in figure 6.23(b), separate read-write heads are used for each surface. The heads are mounted on to a single actuator arm, which moves them to the same track numbers on each surface. Each set of corresponding tracks is referred to as a *cylinder*. The disk (platter), spindle motor and head actuator are usually contained in a sealed chamber called the *head disk assembly* (HDA). The HDA is controlled by a *disk controller*, which specifies the track and sector numbers together with the type of operation (read or write) to be performed.

---

[1] millionth of a metre

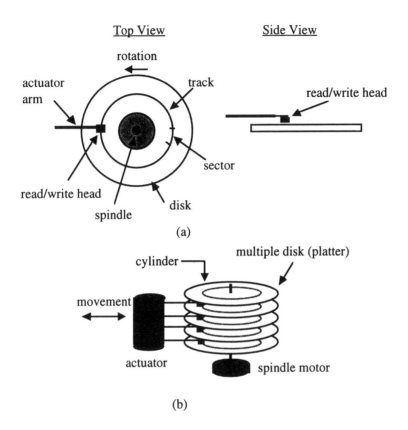

Figure 6.23 Magnetic disk storage

Reading and writing to the disk take place in serial fashion. During a read operation, the controller transfers one or more blocks of data from the disk into a temporary storage area, called a *sector buffer*, a block being typically 512 bytes. During a write operation, the contents of the buffer are transferred serially to the specified track and sector. To assist the controller in these operations each sector contains in addition to data, an address (track, head, sector), synchronisation bytes and error checking information.

To access a particular sector, the head must first be stepped to the appropriate track and time allowed for the appropriate sector to pass underneath it. The time taken to do this is called the *access time* and clearly depends upon the positions of the head, track and sector when the operation begins. When describing disk access times, an average value is normally used, based on the average time taken to step to a track (*seek time*) plus the time taken for a sector to reach the head (*rotational latency*). The average rotational latency is normally assumed to be the time taken for half a revolution of the disk.

TQ 6.8   If a disk rotates at 3600 rpm, what is the average rotational latency?

Currently, most hard drives have between two and ten platters and offer storage capacities of between about 40 Mbytes and 3 Gbytes. Access times vary from between about 8 and 80 ms and the rate at which the drive and controller can send data to the system (data transfer rate) can be close on 10 Mbps[2]. Data is recorded using either *Modified Frequency Modulation* (MFM) or *Run Length Limit* (RLL) encoding schemes. With advances in read/write head technology and more efficient encoding schemes, high capacity magnetic disk storage systems are likely to become smaller and faster.

(3) Optical surface technology

Dynamic optical storage systems store data as a series of variable length *pits*, marked along a spiral track in the surface of a hard disk. To read the data, light is focused on to the disk using a low-power semiconductor laser and the variation in intensity of the reflected light caused when light reflects from a pit, rather than the *land* area between the pits, is used to detect the encoded data. Before considering the optical system that makes this possible, we need to describe some of the wave-like properties of light.

Light propagates through space by the interaction of a magnetic field (B) and an electric field (E). As one field changes or oscillates, it induces changes in the other field and causes the wave to move forwards, as illustrated in figure 6.24(a). The arrows or *vectors* represent the magnitude and direction of the E and B fields as the wave moves along, the vectors being at right angles to each other and to the direction of propagation. The *wavelength* is the distance taken for either field to perform one oscillation and is typically 700 nm for the semiconductor lasers used in optical storage systems. Because the vectors representing the E-field all lie in the same plane, we describe the light wave shown in the figure as *plane polarised*. In contrast, figure 6.24(b) shows an *elliptically polarised* light wave, where the E-field rotates about a circle or ellipse as the wave moves forwards.

---

[2] Mega bits per second

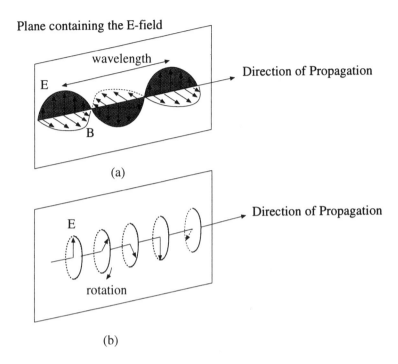

Figure 6.24 (a) Plane polarised (b) Elliptically polarised light

Ordinarily light is *unpolarised*, which means that the E-field has no preferred direction in space and can take up any orientation in a plane perpendicular to the direction of propagation. To convert this to plane polarised light, we use a *polarising prism*, as shown in figure 6.25. The prism is made from *calcite*, which because of its molecular structure, produces two light waves polarised at right angles to each other, when unpolarised light is incident on its face. We call these two waves the *ordinary wave* and the *extraordinary wave*. The ordinary wave is polarised in the same direction as the crystal's optical axis, while the extra-ordinary wave is polarised at right angles to it. Calcite is *birefringent*, which means that its *refractive index* for an ordinary wave is different from that of an extraordinary wave. Because of this, when the two waves arrive at the air gap between the crystals, only the extraordinary wave is transmitted, the ordinary wave being critically reflected.

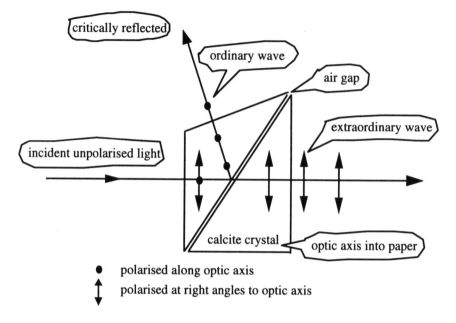

Figure 6.25 Production of plane polarised light

Elliptically polarised light can be produced by passing plane polarised light through a *quarter-wave plate*, made from *mica* or some other *anisotropic crystal*, as shown in figure 6.26(a).

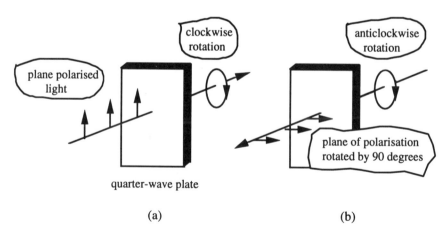

Figure 6.26 Rotating plane polarised light with a quarter-wave plate

When plane polarised light is incident on the plate, the ordinary and extraordinary waves produced travel through the crystal at different speeds. This causes the waves to oscillate out of step or out of *phase* with each other. By arranging the thickness to give a phase difference of 90 degrees, the two waves recombine on the far side of the plate to form elliptically polarised light. The orientation of the incident light relative to the crystal axis, determines whether the transmitted light is elliptically polarised in the clockwise or anticlockwise direction. In figure 6.26(a) we have assumed a clockwise polarisation.

If the elliptically polarised light is now reflected from a surface and passed back through the plate, as shown in figure 6.26(b), then the resulting phase shift converts it back into plane polarised light once again. This time however, the plane of polarised is at 90 degrees to its original direction. The ability of a quarter wave plate to rotate the plane of polarisation in this way is used to separate incident and reflected beams in optical storage systems.

Another wave-like property of light exploited in optical storage systems is *interference*, which occurs when waves are superimposed and added. By the *principle of superposition*, if the two waves are in phase, as shown in figure 6.27(a), then they interfere constructively to produce a new wave having twice the amplitude of an individual wave, whilst if the two waves are in antiphase, as shown in figure 6.27(b), the waves interfere destructively and cancel out.

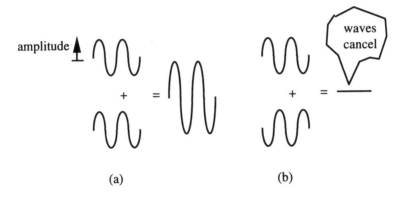

Figure 6.27 (a) Constructive interference (b) Destructive interference

In the next section, we will see how these properties are put to use in various optical storage devices.

(4) CD-ROM

A CD-ROM is a compact disk read-only memory. The disks are mass produced by stamping the pits on to a polycarbonate substrate using special nickel-plated master disks. The substrate is then coated with a thin reflective layer and finally protected from scratching by lacquering. Although master disks are expensive to manufacture and test, each master is capable of stamping out up to 10,000 disks, making CD-ROM storage cost effective for large production runs. Once manufactured, the pattern of pits in the surface of a CD-ROM cannot be altered.

To read the disk, a sophisticated optical system is used, as shown in figure 6.28(a). Light from a low-power laser diode is focused as a spot on to the disk surface, by means of a collimator and an objective lens. Before reaching the disk, the light is plane polarised by a polarising prism, and then converted into elliptically polarised light by a quarter-wave plate. After reflecting back through the quarter-wave plate, because the light is now plane polarised along the optical axis of the polarising prism, it is critically reflected on to the *spot detector* or photo-diode, instead of being transmitted through the prism and back to the laser.

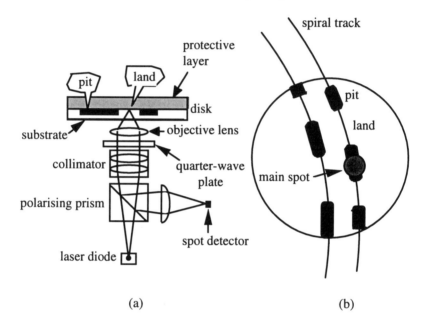

(a)   (b)

Figure 6.28 CD-ROM

When the spot passes over a pit, as shown in figure 6.28(b), the light tends to be scattered, reducing the intensity of the reflected beam. Also, because the pits are only a quarter of a wavelength deep, light reflected from a pit is in antiphase with that reflected from the surrounding land, resulting in *destructive interference* and a reduced reflectivity. In contrast, when the spot passes over the land area between the pits, there is no scattering and *constructive interference* results in a much higher reflectivity. Therefore, as the disk rotates, the light reaching the spot detector is modulated according to the pattern of pits marked in the disk substrate. The signal that this generates can then be processed to extract the encoded data.

Data is stored along the spiral track in *sectors*, where sectors are counted from the centre outwards. Each sector contains 3234 bytes, 882 bytes being used as an *Error Detection Code/Error Correction Code* (EDC/ECC) and also to provide control information. The remaining 2352 bytes are defined according to various *colour book* standards. The CD-ROM Mode 1 *yellow book standard*, allows 2048 of these bytes to be used for data, the remaining bytes being used for synchronisation, header and as an additional EDC/ECC. The 4-byte header contains the address of the sector in minutes:seconds:blocks measured from the beginning of the track.

The number of bits stored per mm of track, or *storage density* of a CD-ROM is about five times that of a magnetic hard disk. The storage capacity of a 120mm disk is 553 Mbytes of user data and the average random access time is between 100-200ms. The average data transfer rate is about 150Kbps and because of the error correction system, the unrecoverable error rate is as low as 1 in 10^{12} bits.

When comparing optical with magnetic surface storage, there are a number of advantages. Firstly, the storage density is about five times that of a magnetic disc and secondly, the optical system used to detect the data is not in contact with the disk surface, being typically about 1mm above it. This eliminates problems caused by debris getting on to the disk surface and allows optical disks to be removed from the drive when not in use or when data needs to be exchanged. In contrast, the heads of hard disk systems, such as Winchester drives, fly extremely close to the disk surface, which means that any dust or dirt on the disk is liable to cause the head to crash into the disk surface and damage it. For this reason, hard disks are assembled under clean-room conditions and then sealed, so that they cannot be removed. Finally, because of the error detection/correction codes used with optical disks, less stringent quality requirements are needed during their manufacture than are needed for hard disks, making them more economical to produce.

(5) WORM devices

Write-Once-Read-Mostly (WORM) optical storage devices, allow users to archive data by storing it on an initially blank optical disk or tape. A popular WORM disk is the Compact Disk-Recordable (CD-R), which has a reflective layer that can be permanently altered and used to store data.

The CD-R drives contain two semiconductor lasers, one for writing and the other for reading data. The laser used for writing has a typical power rating of 30mW, which means that it can heat the surface of the disk to form holes, create bubbles or otherwise alter the reflectivity of the film deposited on it. The laser used for reading has a lower power rating and therefore cannot alter the recorded data. It operates in the same way as the laser diode we described for the CD-ROM.

(6) WREM devices

Write-Read-Erase-Memory (WREM) optical storage devices, also called *magneto-optical memories*, are the optical equivalent of the magnetic hard disk and allow data to be written, read, erased and re-written many times. A typical disk contains a thin magneto-optic film sandwiched between a number of other layers, as shown in figure 6.29(a).

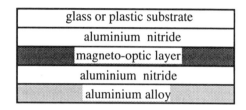

(a)

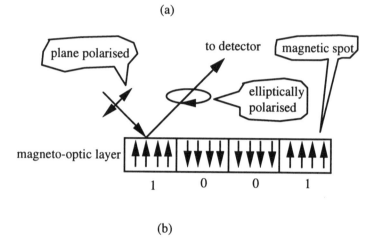

(b)

Figure 6.29 Magneto-optical device

Data is recorded as a series of vertically magnetised spots on the magneto-optic layer, as shown in figure 6.29(b). Each spot is about 1 micron across.

When plane polarised light is directed through the substrate and aluminium nitride layers on to a spot, it is reflected from the magneto-optic layer as elliptically polarised light. This is due to a phenomenon called the *polar-Kerr effect*. The reflected light is elliptically polarised in either a clockwise or anticlockwise direction, depending upon the direction in which the spot is magnetised. Using a suitable optical system, these differences can be measured and used to determine the recorded bit pattern.

Data is recorded by directing high power laser light on to a spot, so that it is heated above its *curie temperature*, which is between 150 and 200°C. At this temperature, magnetic reversals can be induced with an external magnetic field.

Typical commercial 130mm WREM drives offer storage capacities of about 1.3 Gbytes.

6.7 Summary

Computer memory is organised into a hierarchy of different layers, because fast memory technology is more expensive than slower memory technology. A small high-speed cache memory allows the internal memory to 'appear' as high speed memory, by storing a limited number of recently used memory blocks, that by the locality principle, are likely to be used again. Three mapping schemes are used for storing blocks in a cache: associative, direct and set-associative.

Semiconductor technology is used for implementing internal memory, while magnetic surface and optical technologies are used for external secondary storage. Semiconductor technologies include bipolar, MOS, CMOS, HMOS, which are used for implementing SRAM, DRAM and various types of ROM including EPROM and EEPROM. Magnetic surface technology is used for implementing hard disk storage devices while optical technology is used for implementing CD-ROMs, WORM and WREM devices.

6.8 Answers to Text Questions

TQ 6.1 Primary storage: 2000/1024.1024.8 = 0.00024 p/bit
Secondary storage: 10000/200.1024.1024.8 = 0.000006 p/bit
The cost of storing information in primary memory is therefore 40 times more expensive than secondary memory.

TQ 6.2 2^{10} or 1024

TQ 6.3 The bar over the chip select pin indicates that the chip is selected by taking this pin low, in the same way as the bar over the W on the read-write line indicated that the line was taken low for a write operation.

TQ 6.4 Maximum read access time for chip = 500 − 200 − 50 = 250 ns

TQ 6.5 $t_{av} = 0.9 \times 20 + 0.1 \times 80 = 26$ ns
Without a cache memory, (h = 0) and $t_{av} = t_m = 80$ ns.
Therefore the speedup factor is 80/26 = 3.1

TQ 6.6 The tag is FE080 and the word field indicates that the byte occupies position 2 in the block, therefore the cache line entry would be appear as:

FE080 b b <u>7A</u> b b b b b b b b b b b b b   [b's indicate bytes]

TQ 6.7 Address $5A0FF0_{16}$ to $5A0FFF_{16}$

TQ 6.8 Each revolution takes 1/60 seconds.
On average, a sector will be half a revolution away from head, so the rotational latency will be 1/120 or 8 ms.

6.9 Exercises

1.   If a static RAM chip is organised as 2048 x 8 bit, then
       (a) How many bits are stored ?
       (b) How many address pins will it have ?

2.   List the advantages and disadvantages of the three cache mapping schemes
       described in this chapter.

3.   What is the difference between *write-through* and *write-back* when
       describing a cache coherency policy ?
       The access time of a cache memory is 20 ns and that of main memory is
       100 ns. It is estimated that 85% of a program's memory requests are for
       reads and 15% for writes. If the hit-ratio is 0.95, and a write-through
       policy is used, what is the average access time of the system ?

4.   A four-way set associative cache uses a least recently used (LRU)
       replacement algorithm. To support this, each block in the set has two bits
       that are used for counting when the block was last used. The counters work
       as follows:

       •   When a 'miss' occurs, the block whose counter has reached zero is
           replaced by the newly referenced block. On being entered in the cache,
           the counter of this new block is initialised to 3, while all other blocks in
           the set have their counters decremented by 1.

       •   When a 'hit' occurs, the counter of the block containing the referenced
           word is reset to 3. Before this is done, any block whose counter is
           greater than that of the referenced block is decremented by 1, while all
           other counters are left unchanged.

       If the cache currently has the four blocks A, B, C, D in a set, with block
       counters equal to 0, 1, 2, and 3 respectively, then after the following
       sequence of blocks have been referenced: E, B, E, D, A, E, which blocks
       will be in the set and what will their counter values be?

5.   The expression, $t_{av} = ht_c + (1 - h)t_m$ for the average access time of a cache
       does not take into account the time required to transfer a block of words
       into the cache. Measurements show that t_{av} varies with block size as shown
       below.

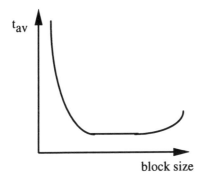

How do you account for this?

6. The following specification refers to a multi-platter hard disk drive:

number of heads	12
number of cylinders	989
rotational speed	3600 rpm
sectors/track	35
bytes/sector	512

(a) What is the storage capacity of the system in Mbytes?
(b) What is the maximum data transfer rate in MB/second?

7. A 74 minute CD-ROM is read at 4500 sectors per minute. How many sectors are there on the disk ? If each 3234 byte sector contains 2048 bytes of data, what is the storage capacity of this disk from the user's point of view? What purpose do the other bytes serve?

8. How many 1.44 Mbyte floppy disks could you store on a 650 Mbyte CD-ROM?

References

Bradley, A (1991), *Peripherals for Computer Systems*, Macmillan Press Ltd.
Byte (1991), *The Incredible Shrinking Disk*, McGraw-Hill Pub, **16**, 10, Oct 91.
Hennessy, J.L, Patterson. D.A (1996), *Computer Architecture A Quantitative Approach*, Morgan Kaufmann Pub Inc, p.429.
Williams, E.W (1994), *The CD-ROM and Optical Disc Recording Systems*, Oxford University Press.

7 Input-Output

Input-Output (IO) is a term used to describe the transfer of information between a computer's main memory and the various IO devices attached to it. These peripheral devices are generally slower than the CPU and frequently require special control signals and data formats. To match these characteristics with those of the CPU and its internal memory, interface circuits are used. This chapter describes the basic principles of microcomputer interfacing and the methods used for scheduling data transfer.

7.1 Types of Interface

Although there are many different types of interface, one important characteristic which distinguishes them is whether they support *parallel* or *serial* data transfer. A *parallel interface* transfers several bits together using a separate data line for each bit, as shown in figure 7.1(a), while a *serial interface* transfers the data bits one at a time over a single data line, as shown in figure 7.1(b).

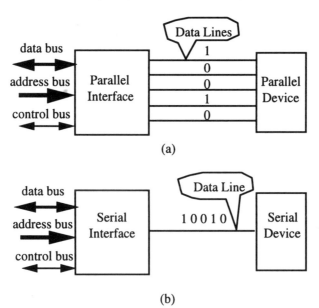

(a)

(b)

Figure 7.1 (a) Parallel (b) Serial Input-Output

Parallel interfaces tend to be used for locally connected high-speed devices, while slower or remotely connected devices are connected by a serial interface.

At a minimum, an interface circuit contains at least a one-word buffer register called an IO *port*. The CPU can address this register and receive or send data by reading/writing to it. The interface handles any necessary data transformations and timing/control that the CPU would otherwise have to carry out itself.

Most microprocessor manufacturers provide several *peripheral support chips* for interfacing IO devices to their systems. These support chips are usually *programmable*, allowing them to be modified under program control to match the characteristics of different IO devices. They can range from relatively simple or 'dumb' circuits that provide just a few basic ports, to more 'intelligent' chips such as disk controllers, capable of moving blocks of data to and from memory, without any intervention by the CPU.

7.2 Parallel IO

A simplified block diagram of a parallel IO interface is shown in figure 7.2.

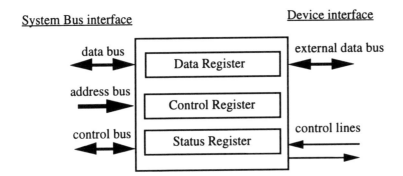

Figure 7.2 Parallel IO interface

The unit has three registers: a *data register*, a *control register* and a *status register*, which the CPU can access over the system bus. The *external data bus* is a collection of parallel data lines, that can be configured as input or output by writing a suitable bit pattern into the *control register*. Once configured, data is transferred to or from this bus by writing/reading the data register or *port*, which acts as a *buffer* between the system bus and the *external data bus*. The *status register* is used to record or flag events, such as device ready and data available. By inspecting this register, the CPU can decide when to send or receive data.

(1) Handshaking

The external data bus must be capable of supporting data transfer with a wide range of different peripheral devices. Because the speeds of these devices are usually unknown, *control* or *handshake signals* are provided to synchronise the bus activities of the interface with those of the IO device.

Figure 7.3 illustrates how *handshaking* is used to transfer data from an output port to a printer. This particular *handshake protocol* uses two control lines, labelled Data Available (DAV) and Data Accepted (DAC). Each control signal is *asserted* by taking its line voltage high (e.g. 5 volts) and *negated* by taking its line voltage low (e.g. 0 volts).

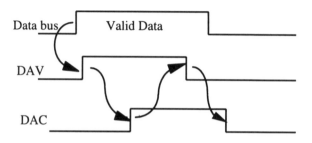

Figure 7.3 Data transfer using handshaking

The handshake is initiated by the interface, which puts data on the data bus and asserts DAV to indicate that new data is available. When the printer detects this signal, it reads the data from the bus and acknowledges its reception by asserting DAC. In response, the interface negates DAV and removes the data from the bus. After processing the data, the printer negates DAC to complete the handshake and to indicate that it is now ready for the next character.

Most IO interfaces allow the control lines to be programmed to suit the needs of a particular device. For example, they can be programmed to provide a *pulsed* handshake or to change an assertion from *active-high* to *active-low*. We will demonstrate this by considering a real interface chip, the Rockwell 6522 Versatile Interface Adapter (VIA).

(2) Rockwell 6522 VIA

This chip, originally developed to provide a pair of parallel IO ports and a timer-shifter for the R6500 processor family, can also be used for interfacing other processors, including the MC68000 we described in chapter 5. Figure 7.4 shows one of the 8-bit ports (Port B) of the 6522, together with the address decoding logic and some of its internal registers.

The 8-bit *input-output* register (ORB) can be configured as an input, output or input/output port by setting/clearing bits in the 8-bit *data direction* register (DDRB). Whenever a particular bit in DDRB is set to '1', the corresponding data line in ORB is configured as output and whenever the bit is set to '0', the corresponding data line is configured as input. Once configured, data is transferred through ORB.

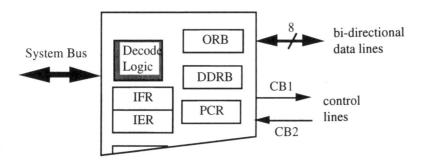

ORB Input/Output Register B
DDRB Data Direction Register B
PCR Peripheral Control Register
IFR Interrupt Flag Register
IER Interrupt Enable Register

Figure 7.4 The 6522 Port B and associated registers

TQ 7.1   How would the port be configured if we stored $FF in DDRB?

The 8-bit *peripheral control* register, shown in figure 7.5, uses bits 4 to 7 to control the type of handshaking signals generated and recognised by the ports CB1 and CB2 control lines. By setting/clearing bit 4, an active-high/active-low output signal is generated on CB1 when data is written into ORB. In a similar way, the CB2 control signal is specified using bits 5 to 7. By clearing these bits, an active-low signal received on CB2 causes a flag to be set in the *interrupt flag* register. This flag is automatically cleared when ORB is read by the CPU.

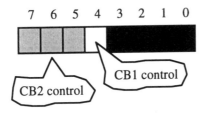

Figure 7.5 Peripheral Control Register (PCR)

The *interrupt enable* register (IER) shown in figure 7.4, is used to enable or disable *interrupts*. We shall return to the topic of interrupts later in the chapter.

7.3 Serial IO

As we mentioned earlier, serial data transfer involves passing data bits one at a time or in *bit-serial form*, over a single data line. Because microcomputers and peripheral devices normally process data in parallel, a serial IO interface must be capable of converting data from *parallel-to-serial* form when transmitting and from *serial-to-parallel* form when receiving. This conversion is performed by *shift registers*, as we discussed in §2.4. Figure 7.6 illustrates how a 3-bit data word could be transmitted and received using a pair of shift registers.

After parallel loading the transmit shift register, the data bits are shifted one after the other on to the data line by the transmit clock. The bits are represented by voltages, such as +12 volts for '0' and −12 volts for a '1'. At the receiver, the bits are sampled and shifted into the register on each cycle of the receive clock.

To recover the transmitted data correctly, the receiver needs to know when to begin sampling the voltage signal and must then keep its clock in step with the transmit clock, at least for the duration of each transmission. We will now discuss how this can be done.

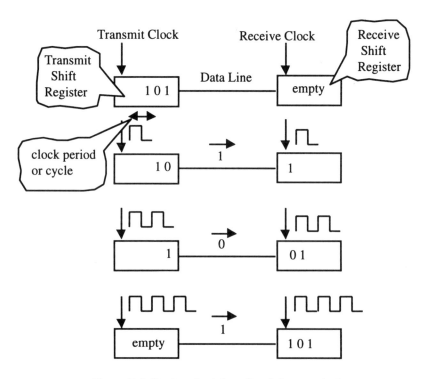

Figure 7.6 Basic principles of serial transmission

(1) Asynchronous serial transmission

With asynchronous transmission, data is transmitted as a series of characters, each character being encapsulated in a *frame*, as shown in figure 7.7. A character frame begins with a start bit and is terminated by one or more stop bits, each character occupying between 5 and 8 bits. The frame also includes an optional *parity bit*, which is used for error detection.

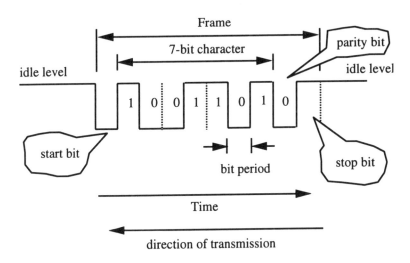

Figure 7.7 Format of a typical asynchronous character frame

The receiver detects the arrival of each frame by its start bit, which takes the voltage on the line from its idle or logic 1 state, down to logic 0. This forces the receiver to reset its clock and begin sampling the data signal at the centre of each bit period. Sampling and shifting continues until a specified number of bits have been received. After checking for the parity and stop bit(s), the receiver transfers the character into its data register. Flags are then set in the receiver's status register to indicate that the data register is full and to report any error conditions.

TQ 7.2　　If we transmitted 100 characters using the frame format shown in figure 7.6, then how many error detection and control bits would we need to send?

Because the receive clock runs independently of the transmit clock, it is possible for a *drift* or change in its frequency to cause the data signal to be sampled 'off centre', as illustrated in figure 7.8.

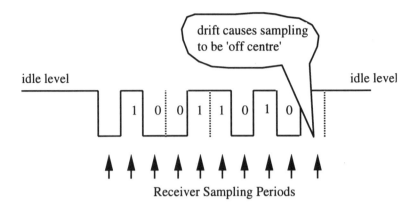

Figure 7.8 Sampling the signal

To reduce the possibility of sampling error, the receive clock is often arranged to run at 16 or 64 times the bit rate of the received data. By doing this, a small change in the frequency of the receive clock will still allow the data to be sampled close to the centre of each bit period.

The speed at which serial data can be transmitted depends upon the frequency at which the voltage signal can change from one level to another. A term often used when describing serial data transmission is the signalling or *baud rate*. The baud rate is the number of signal transitions that can take place in one second. When, as in figure 7.8, a transition represents a change from binary 1 to binary 0, or binary 0 to binary 1, the baud rate is the same as the number of bits transmitted per second or *data rate*.

TQ 7.3   How many characters would we transmit in one second, if our transmission system was operating at 1200 baud?

---

(2) Error detection

Due to the presence of electrical *noise*, there is always a possibility that some of the data bits might become changed or corrupted during transmission. One simple *error detecting* technique is to embed an additional *parity* bit within the transmitted frame before it is sent. If *even parity* is used, the parity bit plus the number of 1s in the character must be an even number, and if odd parity is used, the number of 1s must be an odd number.

TQ 7.4   What form of parity is being used in figure 7.7?

If on receipt of the frame a parity error is detected, then the receiver would flag the event in its status register. This could be used to cause the communication software to take some action, such as requesting a re-transmission.

TQ 7.5   If the character plus parity bit in figure 7.7 is received as 01011010, with the first **two** bits in error, will the error be detected?

Parity checking is only effective when there is a small number of bits and when the probability of a bit error is low.

(3) Asynchronous Communication Interface Adapter (ACIA)

Almost all processor manufacturers offer some form of ACIA, such as the Motorola MC6850. A block diagram of the chip's registers is shown in figure 7.9.

The seven or eight bit word to be transmitted is written into the Transmit Data Register before being shifted out along the Transmit Data Line (TxD). The format of the transmitted frame depends upon bits 2-4 of the 8-bit control word stored in the Control Register, as shown in figure 7.10.

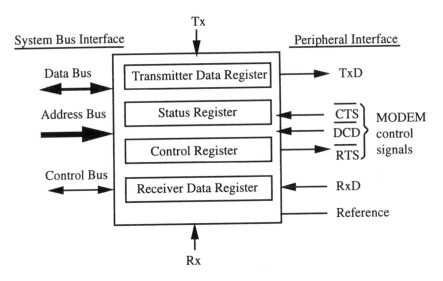

Figure 7.9 MC6850 registers

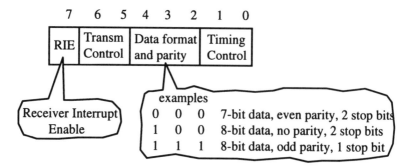

Figure 7.10 Control Register of ACIA

Data is received along the Receive Data Line (RxD) and shifted into the Receive Data Register. Flags are set in the Status Register to indicate when a character has been received and to report any *parity, framing* or *overrun errors*, as shown in figure 7.11. The Status Register is also used to flag interrupt requests, which we will discuss later in the chapter. The Transmit Clock (Tx) and Receive Clock (Rx) provide the necessary timing for transmitting and receiving data. The relationship between the bit rate of the transmission and the frequency of the clocks is determined by bits 0 and 1 in the Control Register.

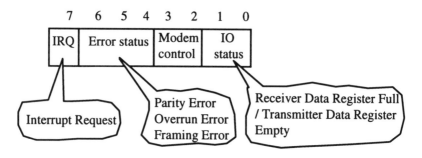

Figure 7.11 Status Register of ACIA

Because the MC6850 has a separate transmitter and receiver, it can send and receive data in both directions at the same time. This mode of operation is called *full-duplex*. Data is normally exchanged at one of the following baud rates: 110, 300, 1200, 2400, 9600 or 19,200 (19.2K).

A MODEM (MOdulator-DEMModulator) is a device that is used to interface a digital system to the public switched telephone network. The control lines: Request-to-Send ($\overline{RTS}$), Clear-to-Send ($\overline{CTS}$) and Data-Carrier-Detect ($\overline{DCD}$) are provided to allow the ACIA to communicate with a MODEM.

(4) Synchronous serial transmission

With *synchronous* transmission, the transmitter and receiver are synchronised to a shared clock and data is transmitted in blocks rather than as individual characters. Figure 7.12 shows a typical bit-oriented synchronous transmission frame.

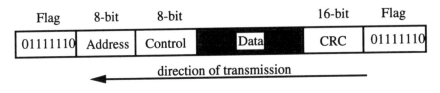

Figure 7.12 Synchronous transmission frame (bit-oriented)

Each frame contains an arbitrary number of data bits, together with a few extra bits for address, control and frame checking (CRC). This bit stream is enclosed by *flag bytes*, to indicate the start and end of a frame. The flags use a special bit pattern that is prevented from occurring in the data by inserting extra 0-bits at the transmitter and deleting them at the receiver. This is called *zero-bit insertion* or *bit stuffing*.

To keep the transmitter and receiver synchronised, timing information is encoded into the bit stream. At the receiver, a clock extraction circuit recovers this information and uses it to provide a clock signal for sampling the data line. Between frames, synchronisation is maintained by transmitting a continuous stream of idle flags.

Because of the reduced amount of control information in each frame, synchronous transmission is more efficient than asynchronous transmission and is used for high-speed data transmission.

7.4 IO Addressing

There are two methods of addressing an IO interface: *memory-mapped* IO and *isolated IO*. The first method assigns portions of the main address space to the registers of each interface, as shown in figure 7.13.

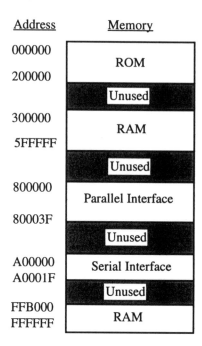

Figure 7.13 Memory-mapped IO

As an example, the data and status registers of a parallel interface might be memory-mapped to hexadecimal addresses 800000 and 800002. These registers can then be accessed using ordinary memory reference instructions. The main disadvantage in doing this is that the address space available for expanding RAM or ROM is reduced. This is usually quite acceptable for a general purpose microcomputer systems with a relatively small IO requirement and is the method used by the Motorola 68000 processor.

With isolated IO, special instructions such as IN and OUT are used to access a separate IO address space. This scheme is used by the Intel 80x86 family of processors. One advantage of using special instructions is that they can be arranged to be *privileged* (see §5.6), so that all IO operations are confined to the operating system.

7.5 Modes of IO Transfer

There are three basic ways of managing or scheduling the transfer of data between memory and an IO device: *programmed IO*, *interrupt-controlled IO* and *Direct Memory Access* (DMA). The extent to which the CPU is actively involved in the transfer depends upon the 'intelligence' of the interface and the particular mode of transfer adopted. We begin our discussion by considering polled or programmed IO.

(1) Programmed IO

With programmed IO, the processor is totally in control of all aspects of the operation. Each data transfer is carried out by executing a polling loop, as illustrated by the flow-chart in figure 7.14.

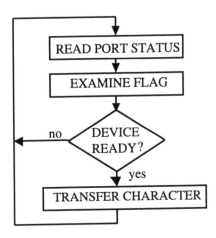

Figure 7.14 Polling loop flow-chart

In this example, the processor schedules the transfer of data to a printer, by first reading the ports status register to see if the printer is able to accept another character. If on examination of this register the 'ready' flag indicates that the printer is busy, the processor loops back and reads the status register again; otherwise, it transfers a character into the data register. Each time data is written to the register, the interface resets the 'ready' flag, and the processor resumes polling on the next character.

A simple program for writing characters to a printer is given in the table 7.1.

Table 7.1 Program for polling a printer port

	ORG	$100	
DR	EQU	$800011	Address of data register
SR	EQU	$80001B	Address of status register
BUFF	EQU	$500000	Address of data area
	LEA	BUFF, A0	A0 points to data buffer area
LOOP	MOVE.B	SR, D0	Read status register
	ANDI.B	#1, D0	Select the 'ready' flag
	BEQ	LOOP	If clear then wait
	MOVE.B	(A0)+,DR	Store character
	BRA	LOOP	Continue

We have assumed that the printer is connected through a parallel port, similar to the one we described earlier. The data and status register are memory-mapped to locations $800011 and $80001B respectively, and bit 0 of the status register is used as a 'ready' flag.

After initialising A0 and moving a copy of the status register into D0, the instruction AND.B #1,D0 is used to *mask off* all bits except bit 0 (see Worked Example in §5.2). If this bit is clear, indicating that the printer is still busy, a conditional branch takes place back to LOOP where the status register is re-examined. If this bit is set, data is transferred to the port by using the instruction MOVE.B (A0)+,DR.

The disadvantage with programmed IO is that the process of checking status bits can waste a lot of otherwise useful processing time, particularly with slow peripheral devices like printers. Even with a relatively fast printer, a processor capable of executing a million instructions per second will often poll a status register about 1000 times before sending a character. Keeping the processor tied up in a polling loop makes poor use of its processing power.

(2) Interrupt-driven IO

A more efficient strategy, called *interrupt-driven* IO, lets the device signal to the processor when it needs servicing. This frees the processor for much of the time and allows it to continue with more useful tasks, such as running other user programs or managing the system's resources.

Interrupts

Virtually all processors have one or more *interrupt request* pins for detecting and recording the arrival of interrupt requests. When an interface or other circuit signals an interrupt, as illustrated in figure 7.15, the processor records the request as pending. Towards the end of each instruction cycle, the processor examines any requests and determines whether to accept and process them, or whether to ignore them and continue executing its current program. The decision depends upon the setting of *interrupt mask* bit(s) in the processor's status register.

When an interrupt is accepted, the processor passes control to an *interrupt handler* or *service routine*, which performs a task, such as sending a character to a printer.

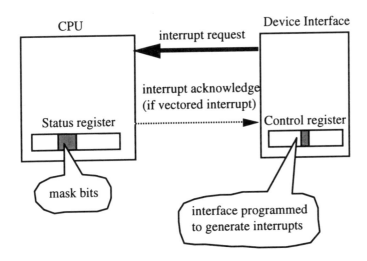

Figure 7.15 Interrupt and possible acknowledgement

Before control is passed to the service routine, the processor preserves the contents of its Program Counter (PC) and Status Register (SR), by pushing them on to the *stack*. It also sets the mask bits in the Status Register to match the *priority level* of the interrupt request, before loading the Program Counter with the start address of the service routine.

For *autovectored* interrupt handling, the start address is found by generating a vector number, the number being related to the priority level indicated by the interrupt request pins. This is used to extract the start address or vector from a table of *exception*[1] *vectors*, which are stored in some fixed memory location.

If *vectored* interrupt handling is used, then after receiving the interrupt, the processor sends an *interrupt acknowledgement* signal (shown by a dashed line in figure 7.15). The device responds by putting a vector number on the data bus, which the processor reads and uses to index the exception table.

After loading the PC with the address of the service routine, the exception handling program is executed until a *ReTurn from Exception* (RTE) instruction is encountered. This instruction *pulls* or *pops* the SR and PC from the stack and passes control back to the interrupted program.

TQ 7.6 In what ways do interrupts differ from subroutine calls?

Prioritised interrupts

When interrupts are generated by a number of different devices, a priority scheme must be used to decide which interrupt should be handled first and whether one

---

[1] an exception is a deviation from the normal activity of the processor

interrupt can interrupt another. The 68000 uses three pins for requesting interrupts: IPL0, IPL1 and IPL2. Normally the pins are held high, a request being made by pulling one or more of the pins low. The priority of the request ranges from level 7 (highest) to level 1 (lowest). A level 7, or *non-maskable* interrupt is generated by taking all three pins low, whilst a level 1 interrupt is generated by asserting IPL0. To arbitrate between simultaneous requests, an interrupt *priority encoder* is usually used, as illustrated in figure 7.16

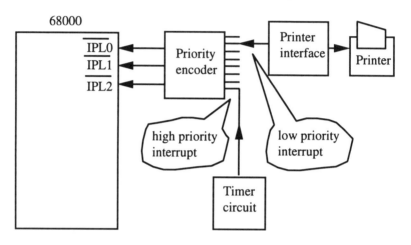

Figure 7.16 Use of priority encoder to handle multiple interrupts

In this illustration, because the system timer interrupt is of a higher priority level than the printer interrupt, then if both devices generate an interrupt simultaneously the priority encoder will only forward the timer interrupt to the processor.

When the 68000 processes an interrupt, it sets its interrupt mask to the same priority level as the interrupt. Any further interrupts are then ignored, unless they have a higher priority than the one being serviced.

It is possible to extend the number of interrupting devices beyond seven by connecting more than one device to the same interrupt line. In such cases, when an interrupt is received, the service routine must identify the source of the request. This is done by examining the status registers of each device in turn to find which device has its *interrupt flag* set. Once found, the service routine selects the appropriate handler.

(3) Direct Memory Access (DMA)

One disadvantage of interrupt-driven IO is that all data transfers involve moving data to and from the processor's registers. Added to this there is the overhead caused by preserving and retrieving the PC, SR and any other registers used by the service routine. For rapid data transfer this can be too slow and an alternative strategy, called *Direct memory Access* (DMA), must be used.

Many device controllers, particularly those used for block devices, support DMA. An example of such a device is a disk controller, which transfers blocks of bytes directly between a hard or floppy disk and main memory, as illustrated in Figure 7.17.

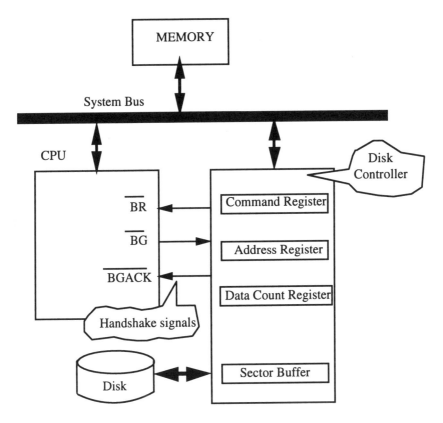

BR = Bus Request; BG = Bus Grant; BGACK = Bus Grant Acknowledge.

Figure 7.17 Disk controller configuration

In §6.6, we described how magnetic disks were divided into tracks and sectors, each sector being used to store a block of data. To read a sector, the CPU first loads the controller's *address register* with the memory address of the data buffer to be used, and the controller's *data count register* with the number of bytes to be read. A few bytes are then written into the *command register* to specify the track, sector numbers and the mode of transfer to be used ('read' in this case).

The controller responds by stepping the read/write head to the appropriate track and reading the serial bit stream from the specified sector into its *sector buffer register.* After reading the block and checking for any errors, the DMA controller copies the buffer into memory, using information provided by the address and data count registers. The controller does this by first gaining control of the system bus through a series of handshakes with the CPU.

As *bus master*, the controller now has full control of the buses and begins writing the bytes one after the other into the address specified in the address register. After each byte is written, the data count register is decremented and the address register incremented. This continues until the data count register reaches zero, at which point, the controller relinquishes control of the buses and hands it back to the CPU. Normally after doing this, the controller generates an interrupt, to inform the CPU that it is ready to be initialised for a further transfer.

The mode of operation we have just described is called *burst transfer mode.* Although this is the fastest mode of I/O transfer, it forces the CPU to idle for the duration of the transfer, which is only acceptable on simple systems. For most systems, it is more efficient for the DMA controller to just slow the CPU down by 'stealing' bus cycles. This method of operation is called *cycle stealing mode.*

In cycle stealing mode, just before the CPU begins a bus cycle, it is suspended, and a single word is transferred by the DMA controller. After regaining control, the CPU then completes the bus cycle, for example by fetching an instruction or reading an operand. It should be noted that suspending the CPU in this way is not the same as interrupting it, as no register preservation needs to be carried out. The overall effect of this mode of transfer is to cause the CPU to slow down, rather than forcing it to temporarily halt.

Even with a DMA controller, there is still a need for CPU intervention after each block is transferred. To reduce CPU involvement, particularly when an operation requires several blocks to be transferred, a more specialised controller or *I/O processor* is used. I/O processors or *channel controllers* can execute a series of I/O instructions in the form of an *I/O program* that is stored either in controller memory or in a fixed area of main memory. The I/O instructions include details of the number and size of blocks to be transferred, which blocks need to be read and written and the transfer addresses involved. Normally this program is set up by the operating system (see §8.1).

7.6 Summary

A peripheral device is connected to a computer system through an interface. The type of interface required depends upon whether the device supports parallel or serial data transmission. Programmable interfaces contain addressable registers for storing data, reporting status information and controlling the way in which the interface operates. Register addresses can be arranged as part of the main memory address space (memory-mapped) or as part of a separate IO address space (isolated-IO).

Peripherals located more than a few metres away from the computer use serial data transmission and require a serial interface, such as a ACIA. Serial data can be transmitted on a character-by-character basis, using asynchronous transmission, or in blocks, using synchronous transmission. Asynchronous transmission is slower and less efficient than synchronous transmission.

Three scheduling strategies are used to control data transfer between peripheral devices and memory: programmed IO, interrupt-driven IO and Direct Memory Access (DMA). Programmed IO is simple but inefficient in terms of processor usage. Interrupt-controlled IO is usually more efficient but is too slow for very fast IO, such as reading or writing blocks of data from a disk. DMA offers the fastest form of IO, using a controller to transfer data directly between main memory and the IO device. DMA can be used in burst transfer mode or cycle stealing mode. Cycle stealing mode is preferred in high performance systems, as it slows the CPU down rather than causing it to stop for the duration of the transfer. To reduce the intervention of the CPU even further, some systems use more intelligent I/O processors or channel controllers.

7.7 Answers to Text Questions

TQ 7.1   The bit pattern stored would be 11111111 and therefore the port would be configured as an 8-bit output port.

TQ 7.2   For each character we need to send one start bit, one stop bit and a parity bit. Therefore to send 100 characters, we need to transmit 30 extra bits.

TQ 7.3   Because the bit rate is the same as the baud rate, then 1200 bps (bits per second) can be transmitted. Each character frame contains 10 bits, therefore the character data rate is 120 cps (characters per second).

TQ 7.4   The total number of 1s in the character plus parity bit is 4. Therefore even parity is being used.

TQ 7.5   With a two bit error, the received data still has even parity and therefore the error will pass undetected.

TQ 7.6   Subroutine calls take place when an instruction is executed, whereas Interrupts are caused by a signal.
Subroutine calls cause only the PC to be pushed on to the stack, while Interrupts preserve both the PC and SR.
Subroutines end with a RTS instruction whereas Interrupt service routines end with a RTE instruction.

7.8 Exercises

1.   By referring to figure 7.7, draw a diagram of an asynchronous character frame when the ASCII character, 'A', is being transmitted. Assume that even parity is used and that the frame is terminated by a single stop bit.

2.   Interrupt service routines can use any of the processor's registers, not just the PC and SR. Why does the processor therefore only preserve these two registers automatically, leaving the task of preserving any other registers to the interrupt service routine?

3.   A keyboard interface is polled 10 times a second, to ensure that all keystrokes entered by the user are captured. If the polling routine occupies 50 clock cycles and the processor is driven by a 100 MHz clock, then what percentage of processing time is wasted by this operation? Why is polling unacceptable for handling disk transfers?

4.   The MC68000 has no dedicated bus or specialised instructions to support IO and relies entirely on memory-mapped IO for transferring data to/from peripheral devices. Discuss the disadvantages of this strategy.

5.   Why is DMA and not interrupt-driven IO used for handling hard disk data transfers? A DMA controller can operate in burst transfer mode or cycle stealing mode. How do these modes differ and why is the latter mode usually preferred?

References

Hennessy, J.L, Patterson. D.A (1994), *Computer Organisation and Design*, Morgan Kaufmann Publishers Inc, pp. 565-582.

8 Operating Systems

An *operating system* is a collection of system programs that manage the resources of a computer and control the running of user programs. The purpose of this chapter is to describe various hardware features that are used to support a typical microcomputer operating system.

8.1 Overview

Microcomputer operating systems are usually stored on hard or floppy disk. When a computer is switched on, the CPU executes a *bootstrap* program, part of which must be held in ROM. This program loads the *kernel* and other frequently needed portions of the operating system into main memory and sets it running by altering the program counter, as illustrated in figure 8.1.

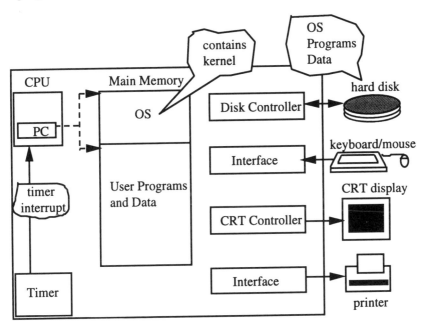

Figure 8.1 Physical resources managed by the operating system

The operating system then sets about creating various tables, lists and other data structures needed to manage the resources of the system. Resources include memory; I/O devices; files; buffers; and the CPU itself. It also sets up vectors in the exception vector table (see §7.5), so that it can provide services to the user. It is then ready to accept commands through a GUI or some other form of user interface.

To execute a user program, the operating system first loads it into main memory and then, after switching from supervisor mode to user mode (see §5.6), hands it control of the CPU by setting the program counter (PC) to the address of its entry point instruction. The user program then runs until either a *system call* (*trap*) or hardware *interrupt* returns control back to a part of the operating system kernel called the *interrupt handler*. Traps and interrupts are examples of *exceptions*, which as we mentioned in the last chapter, are events that alter the normal execution of a program. The interrupt handler is responsible for determining the cause of the exception and for initiating an appropriate service routine.

8.2 Multiprogramming

Many modern operating systems have the ability to execute several programs at once, even though there is often only one CPU or processor in the system. This is called *multiprogramming* and is made possible by rapidly switching the processor between programs. By periodically interrupting the processor, each program is given control of the processor for a short time interval or *quantum*, before being *preempted* by another program. Figure 8.2 indicates how this pro-cess works.

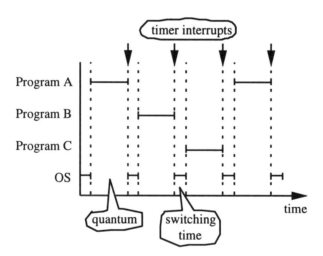

Figure 8.2 CPU time divided between user programs

Switching is triggered by a hardware device called an *interval timer*, which generates a *time-out interrupt* after a programmed period of time has elapsed. Each time-out invokes the interrupt handler, which saves the *context* of the processor before handing over control to a *dispatcher* or *low-level scheduler*. The context includes the Program Counter (PC), Stack Pointer (SP), Status Register (SR) and other processor registers that might be overwritten by other programs.

The dispatcher then searches a list of potentially runnable programs using a *scheduling algorithm* to select a suitable program to run next. It then restores the context of the processor to that which existed when the selected program was last halted and sets it off running again.

To delve any deeper into the inner workings of an operating system, we need to introduce the concept of a *process*.

8.3 The Process Concept

A process, which can be a *user process* or *system process*, consists of an executable program, the data associated with it and an *execution context*. The execution context includes the processor context we have just described, together with other information, such as a process identifier (PID), a priority level and a process state.

There are three basic process states: *Ready*, *Running* and *Blocked*, which we have represented by circles in the state transition diagram shown in figure 8.3.

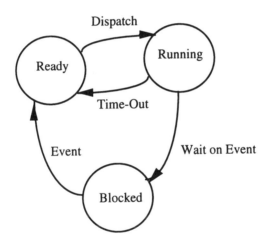

Figure 8.3 State transition diagram

When a user process is in the Running state, the processor is executing its program code. If a timer interrupt occurs, the process is moved into the Ready state and another process is selected from a list of Ready processes and moved into the Running state. If a process in the Running state requests an operating system service for which it must wait, such as an IO request, the process is moved into the Blocked state. The process remains in this state until the event on which it is waiting, such as the arrival of an interrupt from a DMA controller, has taken place. The operating system then moves the process back to the Ready state.

While one process is blocked, awaiting the completion of an IO transfer, the operating system is free to re-schedule another process. This allows the operating system to make efficient use of the computer's limited resources.

TQ 8.1   How does DMA assist in improving efficiency?

8.4 Process Management

When a user initiates the running of a program, a process is created to represent its state of execution. The operating system does this by loading the program code and data into memory and creating a data structure called a *Process Control Block* (PCB), which it uses for management purposes. The structure of a typical PCB is given in figure 8.4.

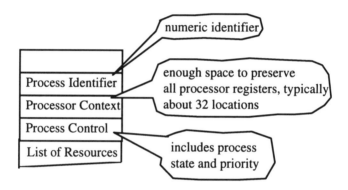

Figure 8.4 Structure of a typical Process Control Block (PCB)

Each PCB has storage space for an identifier; the processor context; process control information; and a list of any resources 'owned' by it, such as files and IO devices. The process control information includes details of the state and priority level of the process, together with information needed for managing memory and interprocess communication.

Before a new process can be scheduled, its PCB must be initialised and added to a list[1] or queue of other Ready processes. This is done by setting the PC entry of the processor context to the start address of the program code and the SP entry to the top of the memory area allocated for its stack. The process control information entries are initialised to various default values, which includes setting the process state to Ready. Figure 8.5 illustrates a typical process queue structure.

---

[1] This is just one way in which an operating system might manage processes

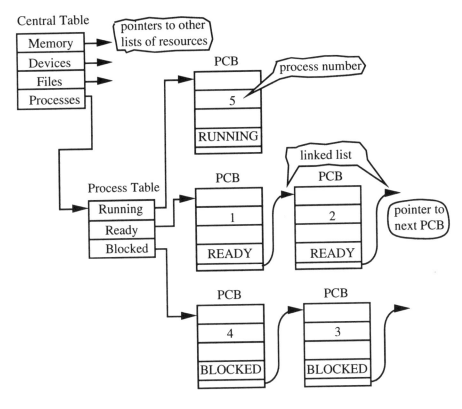

Figure 8.5 Process queue structures

The operating system uses a *central table* to provide access to all the lists and data structures it uses to manage the system. Among its table of pointers is a pointer to a *process table*. The process table has three further pointers: one to the currently running process; another to a list of Ready processes; and a third to a list of Blocked processes. The first PCB in a linked list is said to be at the 'head' of the list.

As processes make transitions between states, their PCBs are updated and moved from one list to another. Only the operating system is allowed to access these data structures, to prevent malicious or accidental damage by user programs. Most operating systems enforce this by running user processes in *user mode* and system processes in *kernel* or *supervisor mode*, as we mentioned earlier. We shall see later that memory management hardware can be used to prevent any attempt by a process in user mode from accessing an area of memory allocated to the operating system.

TQ 8.2   If a time-out occurred and process 1 was chosen to run next, then what changes would be needed to the lists shown in figure 8.5?

TQ 8.3   Sometimes a very low priority process is added to the list of Ready processes that is always able to run. Why is this?

8.5 Process Scheduling

There are several different scheduling algorithms that can be used by the dispatcher. In this section we will consider just two of them: First-Come-First-Served and Round Robin.

(1) First-Come-First-Served (FCFS)

With FCFS scheduling, the process at the head of the Ready list is always the one chosen to run next. Once selected, a process retains control of the CPU until it 'voluntarily' relinquishes it, either by blocking for an IO operation or when the process terminates. This is called *non-preemptive* scheduling. Although this is very simple and easy to implement, it gives unfair advantage to processes that do a lot of calculations with little IO (CPU bound processes). It also suffers from the fact that if a process fails to relinquish control of the CPU, possibly due to a bug in the program, then the whole system is brought to a stand-still. With *preemptive scheduling*, such as Round Robin, this can usually be avoided.

(2) Round Robin (RR)

RR is the form of scheduling we tacitly assumed when we discussed the concept of multiprogramming, a Process being selected from the Ready queue on a FCFS basis and then allocated the CPU for a fixed time quantum. Unlike FCFS, the process is 'forced' to relinquish control of the CPU when its quantum expires and for this reason is described as preemptive scheduling.

The size of the quantum can be altered through program control, a value of 20 ms being quite popular. In choosing the size of the quantum, consideration must be given to typical process interaction times and the types of processes involved. Very short or very long values for the time quantum are always avoided.

TQ 8.4   By referring to figure 8.2, why should a very short quantum be avoided?

8.6 Inter-Process Communication

A process needs to communicate with one or more other processes when competing for shared resources or when cooperating on joint tasks. This section introduces the problems this poses for the operating system and describes some of the methods used to overcome them.

(1) Mutual exclusion

The resources managed by an operating system can be classified as either *physical resources* such as CPU; keyboard; and printer, or *logical resources*, such as shared memory segments and files. A resource is *preemptable* if ownership can be taken away from one process and given to another. If this is not the case, the resource is said to be *non-preemptable* or *critical*.

TQ 8.5   How would you classify a printer?

The section of program code used by a process to access a critical resource is called its *critical section*. Mutual exclusion is concerned with ensuring that, at any moment in time, there can be no more than one process in its critical section on the same resource. This necessitates some form of signalling between competing processes, as we shall see in a moment.

(2) Synchronisation

Another situation in which processes need to communicate is when they need to coordinate their actions. For example, if two processes P_1 and P_2 share a buffer in which P_1 deposits data (*producer*) and P_2 removes data (*consumer*), then steps must be taken to prevent data being consumed when the buffer is empty and to prevent data being produced when the buffer is full. Once again, some form of signalling is needed between the processes.

(3) Achieving mutual exclusion

As a first approach to implementing mutual exclusion, let us consider using a variable called *flag*, to indicate when a resource is available (*flag* = 0) or in use (*flag* = 1). The following pseudocode illustrates how a flag could be used by a process to gain access to a critical resource.

```
begin
    repeat
        read flag
    until flag = 0
    set flag to 1;
    < Critical Section >
    set flag to 0;
end
```

After examining the flag and finding the resource free (*flag* = 0), the process sets the flag (*flag* = 1) and enter its critical section. If a second process now tried to gain access to the resource, then finding the flag set it would be effectively locked out, and remain in the repeat loop until the flag changed. We describe a process in this condition as *busy-waiting*. When the first process finishes using the resource and leaves its critical section, it clears the flag (*flag* = 0) allowing the second process to gain access.

Unfortunately, this first approach has a fatal flaw, which we can illustrate with the following scenario.

1. Process P_1 examines the flag and finds it free. Just as it is about to set the flag, it is preempted by another process P_2 which also wants to access the resource.

2. P_2 examines the flag and finding it free, sets the flag and enters its critical section. Before it manages to finish with the resource, it too gets preempted and P_1 is re-scheduled.

3. P_1 now proceeds from the point where it was last preempted, by setting the flag and entering its critical section.

   P_1 and P_2 are now both in their critical section and mutual exclusion has been violated!

TQ 8.6   What are the basic causes of this problem?

Hardware support

One hardware solution to the above problem, is to 'turn off' all interrupts before testing and setting the flag. For the MC68000 this can effectively be done by altering the priority level of the process code to level 7 (see §7.5), using an instruction such as:

ORI.W   #0700, SR   OR Immediate data constant $0700 with bits
                          (0:15) of the Status Register

Unfortunately, this can only be used for system processes, because all 68000 instructions that alter the Status Register are *privileged*. This mechanism therefore only provides a partial solution to the problem.

A second solution is to use instructions that can read, modify and write-back a stored variable in a single *indivisible* operation. The 68000 provides such an instruction, called *Test And Set* (TAS). The TAS instruction operates upon a byte sized operand, which it tests before setting the most significant bit (bit-7) to 1. If during this test the byte is found to be negative or zero, then the N and Z flags of the CCR are set. The following assembly code illustrates how the TAS instruction can be used to implement mutual exclusion.

Wait	TAS	flag	
	BNE	Wait	busy-wait
Enter	......		
	......		Critical Section
Exit	MOVE.B	#0, flag	

Although this technique works, it introduces the possibility of another problem called *deadlock*. To illustrate deadlock, consider the following scenario, where we assume the dispatcher uses a priority scheduling algorithm.

1. A low priority process, P_L, is in its critical section on a resource.

2. The dispatcher schedules a process P_H, that has a higher priority than P_L.

3. The dispatcher continues to schedule processes, but never chooses P_L because P_H is always able to run.

Neither process can make any more progress because deadlock has occurred!

TQ 8.7   Would this problem have occurred with RR scheduling?

Software support

To eliminate the need for hardware support, several purely software solutions exist for implementing mutual exclusion. These are based on various algorithms, such as Dekker's algorithm and Peterson's algorithm. As with the hardware solutions, software solutions continue to impose 'busy-waiting' conditions on processes and are prone to deadlock.

(4) Semaphores

A *semaphore* is a flag, bit or combination of bits, used to signal various events, such as whether a resource is free/in-use or whether a buffer is empty/full. In some systems semaphores are implemented in hardware, while in others they are implemented as software constructs (usually non-negative integer variables). A *binary semaphore* can have just two values, 0 or 1, while a *counting semaphore* can have values between 0 and N, where N is a positive integer. If the semaphore is a non-zero positive value, the resource is available and if the semaphore is zero, then it is unavailable. Semaphores are stored in the operating system's address space and accessed by a running process through the primitives[2] **signal** and **wait**. The operating system implements these system calls as *indivisible* or *atomic* operations, possibly by turning off interrupts or using the TAS instruction we described earlier. The operations on a semaphore, s, are defined below.

wait (s):   **if** $(s > 0)$ **then** $(s := s - 1)$
                else add process to queue of processes blocked on s

signal (s):   **if** queue is empty **then** $(s := s + 1)$
                else move a process from queue into the Ready state

To illustrate the use of semaphores, let us consider how they can be used to implement mutual exclusion. We shall assume that the resource is initially available $(s = 1)$.

The first process to request access, P_1, performs a wait(s) and enters its critical section. The execution of wait(s) decrements s, so that $(s = 0)$. If a competing process, P_2, is now scheduled, then on performing wait(s) it gets blocked. When P_1 is re-scheduled, it completes its critical section and executes signal(s). This causes P_2 to be moved back into the Ready state, so that when it is re-scheduled it has immediate access to the resource and enters its critical section. If by the time P_2 is finished there are no further processes blocked on (s), then when it performs signal(s), s is incremented $(s = 1)$ to indicate that the resource is free for use.

---

[2] Very basic processing steps, often consisting of moving or altering bits

TQ 8.8	How does the use of semaphores overcome the 'busy-wait' problem we mentioned earlier?

(5) Other techniques

There are other techniques used for inter-process communication, such as monitors and message passing. We will discuss message passing, when we consider multi-processor systems in chapter 10.

8.7 Memory Management

In our discussion so far, we have tacitly assumed that all the processes known to the system can be stored together in main memory. In reality, due to its finite size, this is not usually possible and is in fact impossible when the size of an individual process exceeds that of main memory. We have also glossed over other issues, such as how one process is prevented from interfering with another and how processes are able to share common areas of memory, such as a buffers. Many modern microcomputer systems overcome these problems by using a technique called *virtual memory*.

(1) Virtual memory

With this technique, addresses generated by the CPU are not used to access main memory directly, but are converted or *mapped* into real addresses which can be either main memory locations, secondary memory locations, or a mixture of both. This allows main memory to be treated as a form of 'cache' for the secondary storage device (usually magnetic disk), mapping only those portions of a program currently required for execution into main memory and keeping the rest of the program on disk until needed. This is illustrated in figure 8.6.

As a program runs, the activity of swapping pieces of code or data in and out of main memory is controlled by a part of the operating system called the *memory management system*. The programmer is unaware of this activity and sees his or her program as occupying a set of memory locations in a logical or *virtual address space*, the details of the *physical address space* it occupies being invisible.

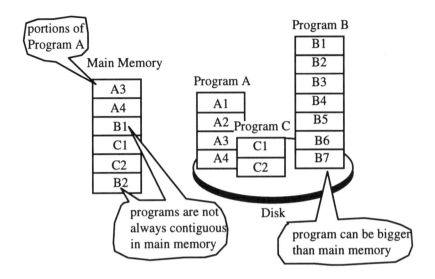

Figure 8.6 Virtual memory concept

TQ 8.9   In chapter 6, we introduced a general property of program behaviour called the *principle of locality*. How does this apply here?

Because all memory references made in a program refer to a virtual address space, then when a CPU executes an instruction such as:

MOVE.B $002003, D0

the address $002003, generated by the CPU, is not the physical address in which the byte is stored but its virtual address. To map this into a physical address requires some form of address translation, as illustrated in figure 8.7.

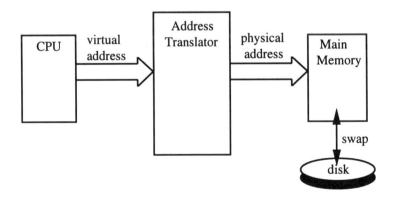

Figure 8.7 Mapping a virtual address to a physical address

If the byte is in memory, then it can be fetched along the data bus and moved into D0 in the usual way. However, if the address translator indicates that the byte is not in memory, then the memory manager must swap a new portion of data from disk into main memory before the byte can be read.

(2) Paging

Most virtual memory systems use an address translation technique called *paging*. With paging, each program is divided into equal size portions called pages, typically between 512 and 4096 bytes. Main memory is also divided up in the same way, but this time into *page frames*, each page frame being capable of storing one page. Virtual addresses generated by the CPU are split into a page number (n) and an offset (d) within the page, while each physical address is split into a frame number (f) and an offset (d) within the frame. A page table is used to map the virtual address into a physical address, as shown in figure 8.8.

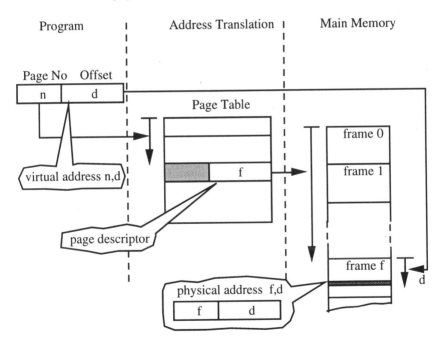

Figure 8.8 Using a page table to perform address translation

The table contains a list of *page descriptors*, each descriptor having a number of bits which describe and control access to the page (shown shaded), together with a frame number (f). The page number (n) of the virtual address (n,d), is used to index the table and identify the frame number (f) into which the page is mapped. The frame number is then combined with the offset (d) of the virtual address, to form the physical address (f,d).

TQ 8.10   A 24-bit virtual address, $002003, has a 12-bit page number (002) and a 12-bit offset (003). If the first few page table entries are as shown below, then to what physical address would this correspond?

Page Table

000	05
001	00
002	01
003	FF
004	0A

Included among the control bits of a page descriptor is a *present bit*, P, which is used to indicate whether the page is in main memory and a *modified* or *dirty bit*, M, to indicate whether the page has been altered. If during an address translation, the P-bit indicates that the page is absent, then a trap to the operating system or *page fault* occurs and a service routine is invoked to load the page from disk. In such cases the virtual address is used to determine the location of the page on disk. Once the page is loaded and the page table updated, then address translation can proceed in the normal way. If there are no spare page frames for the new page, a page must be selected for replacement using some *page replacement algorithm*. We call this form of paging *demand paging*. If the selected page has been modified (M = 1), then before it is overwritten it must be copied back on to the disk.

TQ 8.11   If a page frame used for program code was demanded, then would it need to be copied back to the disk ?

Some page frames, such as those used by the operating system kernel, must be kept permanently in memory. To prevent these frames from being paged out, each descriptor also includes a *lock bit*.

Because page tables are stored in memory, they can also be subjected to paging, especially when they are large. Unfortunately, the additional overhead of swapping portions of the table to and from disk before an address can be translated can add a significant time penalty to this process.

(3) Hardware support for memory management

When paging is implemented without hardware support, then at least two mem-ory accesses are needed to gain access to an instruction: one to read the page table entry and the other to read the instruction. This effectively doubles the memory access time, making virtual memory systems potentially much slower than systems that address memory directly. To reduce this overhead, most virtual memory systems are supported by hardware.

Figure 8.9 shows how a paged *Memory Management Unit* (MMU) is used to translate a virtual address generated into a physical address.

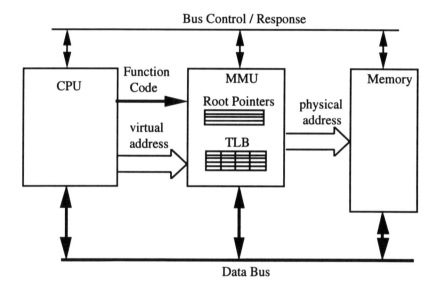

Figure 8.9 Memory Management Unit (MMU)

The MMU reduces the translation time by using a small set-associative address translation cache or *Translation Lookaside Buffer* (TLB). The TLB contains copies of recently used page table entries and can be searched very quickly (see §6.5 on cache memory operation) to find the appropriate descriptor. If the entry is not present, then the MMU takes control of the system bus and uses one of the *root pointers* to access main memory and retrieve the entry from the stored page table. It then updates the TLB before using the page frame to generate the physical address in the usual way. If a page fault occurs, then the page is fetched from disk and the page table updated before repeating the search. A summary of the main steps involved is shown in figure 8.10.

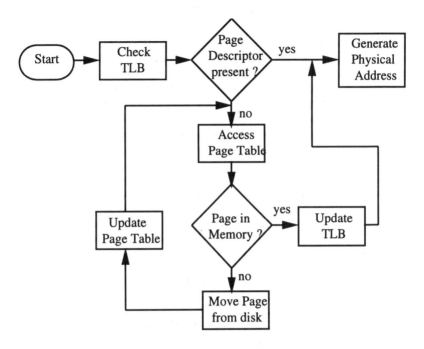

Figure 8.10 Flow-chart for the MMU operation

Most programs only use a few relatively small segments of their virtual address space. A typical program would probably have a one program *code segment*, a *data segment* or *heap* and a *stack segment*. Parts of the heap would probably be shared with other programs and also possibly some of the code segment. To support this type of program structure and to provide a more flexible form of paging, some MMUs use *multi-level page tables*, as illustrated in figure 8.11.

With this two-level scheme, the virtual address is divided into three fields: an A-field; a B-field; and an offset field. The A-field is used to index a set of memory pointers contained in the A-table and locate a set of page descriptors held in the B-table. The B-table is then indexed to find the page frame needed to generate the corresponding physical address.

The location of the A-table is provided by one of the root pointers, selected by the function code generated by the CPU (see figure 8.9). The function code indicates whether the CPU is in user mode or supervisor mode and also the type of cycle (instruction or data) it is currently undertaking. This allows the MMU to select separate A-tables for user code, user data, system code and system data. In this way any invalid operations, such as attempting to write to the user code area, which is designated as read only, can be intercepted and prevented from occurring by trapping to the operating system. The MMU can also provide protection by checking bits in the page descriptor, such as a supervisor only bit, to see if a user is attempting to access an area of memory used by the operating system. It can also support sharing, by allowing multiple entries in the A-tables of different processes to point at the same entry in the B-table.

Logical Address

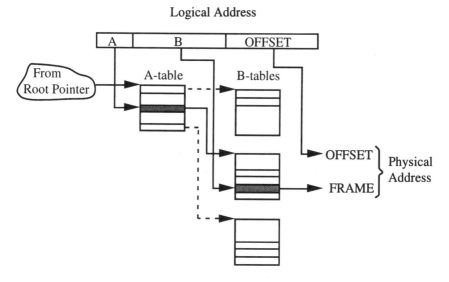

Figure 8.11 Two-level page table

Some MMUs, such as the MC68851, can be programmed to allow three or four different levels of paging, giving even greater flexibility to this type of implementation.

8.8 Summary

In this chapter we have introduced several key features of an operating system and explained how it provides services and manages the resources of the system. We explained the concept of a process and described how an operating system, with the aid of an interrupt handler and dispatcher, can support multiprogramming. The need for process synchronisation and mutual exclusion were then discussed together with two forms of hardware support. Semaphores were then introduced as a mechanism for synchronising processes and for enforcing mutual exclusion, together with the primitive operations, wait and signal. We then discussed memory management and introduced the concepts of virtual and physical address spaces and explained how a page table could be used to map virtual addresses into physical addresses. Finally we described how hardware support, in the form of a paged Memory Management Unit, could be used to assist the operating system in performing this task.

8.9 Answers to Text Questions

TQ 8.1   DMA allows IO to take place without the intervention of the processor. Therefore one process can be running on the processor while another is performing an IO operation in parallel with it.

TQ 8.2   The PCB for process 5 would be updated to Ready and added to the Ready list. The PCB for process 1 would be updated to Running and replace process 5.

TQ 8.3   To prevent the scheduler from running out of processes and halting.

TQ 8.4   If the time quantum approaches the switching time, then the CPU spends more time switching than it does performing the useful work of running processes.

TQ 8.5   A printer is a critical resource, because once a process has started to print a file, it cannot be assigned to another process until the complete file has been printed.

TQ 8.6   a) A process can be interrupted at any time.
          b) Testing and Setting the flag is performed in two operations.

TQ 8.7   No, because RR scheduling makes the implicit assumption that all processes have equal priority.

TQ 8.8   By blocking these processes.

TQ 8.9   The principle of locality refers to the fact that during program execution, certain localised groups of instructions tend to be referenced much more frequently than others. By keeping these portions of a program in main memory and the rest of the program on disk, a reasonable performance can be expected with only occasional delays caused by page swapping.

TQ 8.10   The frame number corresponding to page number 002 is 01. Therefore the physical address would be $01003.

TQ 8.11   No, program code is not modifiable and therefore could not have been changed.

8.10 Exercises

1. What is the difference between a process and a program?

2. Draw a diagram to explain the various state changes a process goes through from the time it is first created.

3. If the time quantum used in Round Robin scheduling becomes too large, then what form of scheduling takes place?

4. How does preemptive scheduling differ from non-preemptive scheduling?

5. Explain the terms critical resource, critical section and mutual exclusion. In what ways can hardware be used to guarantee mutual exclusion?

6. What is a semaphore and what advantages does it offer when used to implement mutual exclusion?

7. A computer using virtual memory has a main memory with just 4 page frames. If the following sequence of virtual page numbers is encountered:

    0 1 2 3 4 3 2 5 6 3 4 5 6 3 5 0

    then if a Least-Recently-Used page replacement policy is used, how many page faults will occur?

8. What purpose does a Translation Lookaside Buffer serve in a Memory Management Unit? Why should caching be disabled on those pages that contain memory-mapped IO device registers?
    [Hint: consider programmed IO that we discussed in §7.5]

References

Heath, S (1993), *Microprocessor Architectures and Systems RISC, CISC & DSP,* Butterworth-Heinemann Ltd.
Lister, A.M, Eager, R.D (1993), *Fundamentals of Operating Systems*, 5th Ed, Macmillan Press Ltd.
Stallings, W (1992), *Operating Systems,* Macmillan Publishing Company.
Theaker, C.J, Brookes G.R (1993), *Concepts of Operating Systems*, Macmillan Press Ltd.

9 Reduced Instruction Set Computers

Two of the best known families of microprocessor are those based on the Motorola 68000 and Intel 8086 architectures, the 680x0 family gaining notoriety through its association with the Apple Macintosh and the 80x86 family through association with the IBM PC. By adopting this family approach, first introduced for IBM mainframes in the mid-sixties, processor designers have been able to take advantage of the implementation techniques and speed increases offered by advances in Very Large Scale Integration (VLSI) technology, while continuing to support a common architecture. Supporting a common architecture is important because it allows software written for older machines to run on newer ones and thus protects the customers' software investment.

Being locked into a particular architecture, designers have tended to increase the power of their processors by increasing the size and complexity of the instruction sets and by adding new features, such as 'on-chip' caches; MMU's; and floating point coprocessor units. In principle, increasing the power of the instruction set eases the burden on the compiler writer and allows shorter and more efficient code to be generated; this is because shorter code reduces the number of memory fetches and hence the processor-memory bottleneck. It also occupies less memory and therefore reduces the number of page faults generated by the MMU.

Based on research, first started in the late 1970s with the IBM 801 project, designers began to question this 'complex instruction set' approach to processor design, particularly after overwhelming evidence suggested that only a small subset of most instruction sets was ever used by compilers. Over the past decade this research has culminated in the emergence of a new breed of commercial machines called Reduced Instruction Set Computers (RISC). This name arises because these processors use a much smaller streamlined instruction set than their Complex Instruction Set Computer (CISC) rivals. At this moment in time, virtually all CISC manufacturers have developed at least one RISC chip, which is a good indication of the importance of the RISC approach in building high speed machines. In this chapter, we examine the philosophy that underpins this approach and give some examples of its implementation.

9.1 CISC Characteristics

Although there is no precise definition of a CISC processor, most of them share the following characteristics:

156

1. A large number of instructions - typically between 100 and 250.

2. Instructions that perform specialised tasks together with instructions that support memory-to-memory operations.

3. A large number of addressing modes - typically between 5 and 20.

4. A range of variable length instruction formats with variable execution times.

5. A microprogrammed control unit.

9.2 Instruction Usage

Because RISC and CISC processors are designed to support the execution of programs written in high-level languages (HLLs), the interaction of compilers with HLLs significantly affects the way in which the processor's instruction set is used. Several studies on CISC instruction set usage have revealed that only a relatively small portion of the instruction set is ever used by CISC compilers. For example, one report [Klein 89] found that roughly 71% of the MC68020 instruction set was not used when a variety of programs were compiled using Sun and Gnu C-compilers. Although the actual instruction usage depends upon factors such as the language and type of program, there is clear evidence that certain types of instruction are used far more frequently than others, as exemplified in table 9.1.

Table 9.1 Typical CISC instruction usage

Instruction type	Average usage
Data Movement	46.3%
Branch and Subroutine Call/Returns	27.6%
Arithmetic	14.1%
Compare	10.4%
Logic	1.6%

Thus HLL assignment statements, such as A := B, which are implemented using data movement primitives like MOVE B,A are used more frequently than logical AND or OR instructions. Also of importance are program modification instructions, such as Branch and Jump instructions, which are used to support HLL iteration in the form of WHILE and FOR loops and also for calling procedures.

Other studies carried out on the use of program variables indicate that the majority of operands accessed by HLL programs are of the single or *scalar* type and that over 80% of these are local procedure variables.

Based on this evidence, processor designers began to develop new architectures designed to be highly efficient in supporting a small (reduced) set of regular instructions and addressing modes, together with efficient ways of storing and retrieving simple operands.

9.3 RISC Architectures

The following characteristics are typical of pure RISC architectures:

1. Relatively few instructions, with single-cycle instruction execution.

2. Relatively few addressing modes.

3. Fixed-length easily decodable instruction formats.

4. Memory access is limited to LOAD and STORE instructions.

5. Relatively large general purpose register sets.

6. Instructions that operate upon operands stored in registers rather than in main memory.

7. A hardwired control unit.

Other characteristics, not exclusively attributed to RISC are:

8. Extensive use of pipelining, including instruction pipelining.

9. Powerful compilers to optimise program code and make good use of the pipelined architecture.

10. Complex functions implemented in software rather than hardware.

TQ 9.1   If a program was compiled to run on a RISC machine, would you expect it to be longer or shorter than if it was compiled to run on a CISC machine?

---

(1) MIPS R3000

The R3000 32-bit RISC processor has 32 × 32-bit general purpose registers. It also has a 32-bit Program Counter and two 32-bit registers for holding the results of integer multiply and divide operations. All R3000 instructions are 32-bits long and there are only three instruction formats to simplify decoding. These formats are shown in figure 9.1.

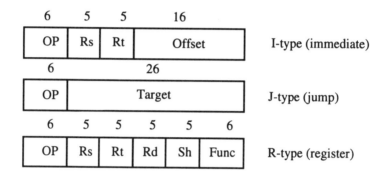

OP = operation code; Rs = source register; Rd = desination register;
Rt = source or destination register; Offset = immediate data, branch or address displacement; Target = target address;
Sh = 5-bit shift amount; Func = ALU/shift function specifier.

Figure 9.1 MIPS R3000 instruction formats

All formats have a 6-bit opcode to specify the operation and the particular format to be used.

The R3000 supports a *Load/Store architecture*, as only Load and Store instructions are used to access memory. Load and Store instructions use the I-format to move data between main memory and the processor's registers.

Example

lb   Rt, address   Load the byte at address into register Rt and sign extend it by 1 byte.
The addressing mode used is base register (Rs) plus 16-bit signed immediate offset.

	6	5	5	16
instruction format	24	Rs	Rt	Offset

Jump instructions use the J-format, as shown below.

Example

j   label   Jump unconditionally to address label.
                          The address is found by shifting the target field 2
                          bits and then combining it with the upper 4-bit of
                          the Program Counter.

6	26
2	Target

instruction format

Computational instructions can use either the I-format or the R-format, as shown in the following examples.

Examples

add   Rd, Rs, Rt   Add the contents of registers Rs and Rt and
                            copy the result into Rd.

6	5	5	5	5	6
0	Rs	Rt	Rd	0	20

instruction format

addi   Rt, Rs, Imm   Add the immediate 16-bit signed literal to the
                            contents of register Rs and copy the result into
                            Rt.

6	5	5	16
8	Rs	Rt	Imm

instruction format

TQ 9.2   How do the instruction formats of the 68000 (see §5.4) compare with
           those of the R3000?

The R3000 uses 74 instructions: 58 basic integer instructions, as shown in table 9.2, together with several others to support coprocessor and system control.

Table 9.2 MIPS R3000 integer instruction types

Instruction type	Number
Load/Store	12
Jump and Branch	12
Arithmetic and Logic	18
Multiply/Divide	8
Shift	6
System Call/Break	2

(2) The memory bottleneck

One of the major problems with von Neumann style machines is the bottleneck caused by the processor-memory interface. This bottleneck arises because main memory is slower than the speed at which the processor can manipulate and process data internally. We can illustrate this by considering the instruction cycle timing for an ADD instruction, using figures taken from a hypothetical computer described in [Gorsline 86]. We assume that one of the operands to be added is stored in memory.

[MAR]	←	[PC]	25 ns
[PC]	←	[PC]+2	25 ns
[MBR]	←	[M([MAR])]	200 ns
[IR]	←	[MBR]	25 ns
Decode Instruction			50 ns
[MAR]	←	Operand Address	25 ns
[MBR]	←	[M([MAR])]	200 ns
Add Operation + set flags			150 ns
Test exceptions			25 ns
		TOTAL	725 ns

TQ 9.3   How much time is taken up accessing memory?

Although the actual time taken for each sub-operation depends upon the VLSI technology used, we can still see that a substantial fraction of each instruction cycle is dominated by the memory access time.

The fact that RISC systems have large sets of general purpose registers and use register-register and not register-memory operations for computational tasks, tends to alleviate this bottleneck and reduces instruction execution time. Also, because RISC instructions are equal to the width of the data bus, each instruction can be fetched in one *memory cycle*, unlike many CISC instructions that often need to be fetched using multiple memory cycles. To reduce the effect of the bottleneck even further, processor designers have adopted various strategies including increasing the width of the data bus to increase the rate at which information is read or written to memory (*memory bandwidth*) and by using caching techniques, as we described in §6.5. Some designers have also resorted to using separate memories for instructions and data, called a *Harvard Architecture*, each memory being served by a separate address and data bus.

(3) *Parameter passing*

The fact that programs tend to make extensive use of procedure call/returns has led some RISC designers to include hardware support for parameter passing between procedures. Processors based on the open RISC architecture specification, called SPARC (Scalable Processor ARChitecture), manage this through the use of overlapping *register windows*. A SPARC implementation may have up to 520×32-bit registers, partitioned into as many as 32 register windows.

Each window consists of 32 registers, only one window being 'visible' or active at a time, as shown in figure 9.2. Procedure B occupies the active window, which is pointed to by a 5-bit *Current Window Pointer* (CWP). Registers R16,..,R23 are used to store local variables, while registers R0,..,R7 hold global variables that are visible to any active procedure.

If Procedure B wishes to pass parameters to Procedure C, then it first copies them in registers R8,..,R15 before calling it. Decrementing CWP on entry to Procedure C, causes the window to slide 'upwards', exposing a new set of register R16,..,R23 and with registers R8,..,R15 becoming R24,..,R31 in the called procedure. When a return is made, the same registers R24,..,R31 are used to pass parameters back to the parent procedure, the CWP being incremented on exit from the procedure.

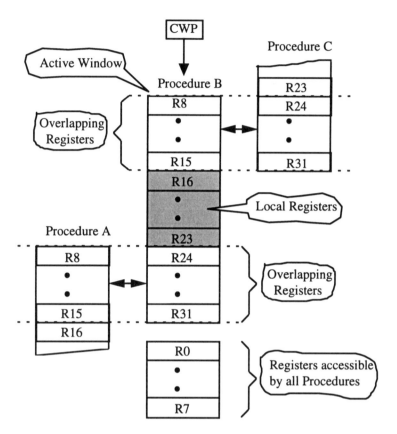

Figure 9.2 Parameter passing using SPARCs register window

TQ 9.4   Why can the SPARC processor only have 32 windows?

In contrast to SPARC architectures, the MIPS R3000 architecture does not provide hardware support for procedure call/returns; instead, it passes the job upwards to its *optimising compiler*. Using special optimisation techniques, such as *procedure merging*, which replaces the call by the procedure code itself, the compiler can either eliminate or at least alleviate the problem. This illustrates the special role that compilers play in RISC systems.

9.4 The Control Unit

In chapter 4, we described the internal organisation of a typical von Neumann style CPU and illustrated how the *control unit* sequenced the flow of data between the various registers and the ALU, which we call the *data path*. One important characteristic that tends to distinguish RISC from CISC architectures, is the implementation of the control unit. Due to the complexity of their instruction sets, CISC designs use a *microprogrammed* control unit, while RISC designs are able to take advantage of a simpler and faster *hardwired* control unit. In this section we compare the basic differences between these control units.

(1) Microprogrammed control unit

The general arrangement of a microprogrammed control unit is shown in figure 9.3. In many ways a microprogrammed control unit is like a CPU within a CPU, having its own *microinstruction Program Counter* which it uses to access a *microprogram* stored in a ROM or *Programmed Logic Array* (PLA). A microprogram consists of a set of *microinstructions*, each microinstruction having a bit pattern which controls the movement of information through the data path. As with machine code or *macroinstructions*, there are Branch and Jump instructions to alter program flow and influence the order in which micro-instructions are executed.

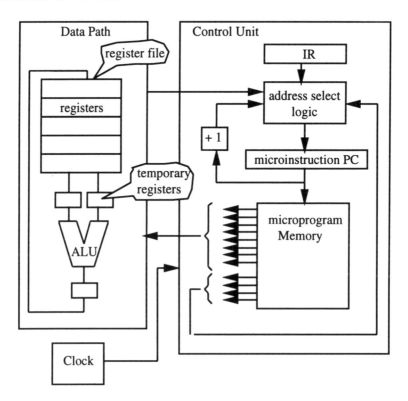

Figure 9.3 Microprogrammed control unit

After an instruction has been fetched into the *instruction register* (IR), decoding begins when the *address   select* or *sequencing logic* identifies the address of the first microinstruction and transfers it to the microinstruction PC. Each microinstruction is an encoded representation of a *microoperation*, which when executed, issues control signals to the data path. The microinstruction also issues signals to the address select logic, which when combined with bits reflecting the state of the data path, generates the address of the next instruction.

The use of *microsubroutines* is a feature included in several microprogrammed control units, because many microprograms require common sequences of microoperations which only need to be included at one place in memory. This reduces the size of the microprogram memory space and helps to reduce the silicon 'real estate' occupied by the control unit. One disadvantage in doing this is that some of these microinstructions may perform redundant operations, which adds to the execution time of the instructions.

There are other ways in which a microprogrammed control unit can be constructed, but we shall not consider them in this book. The main points to noted about a microprogrammed control unit are:

1. They are flexible and allow designers to incorporate new and more powerful instructions as VLSI technology increases the available chip area for the CPU.

2. They allow any design errors discovered during the prototyping stage to be removed.

3. They require several clock cycles to execute each instruction, due to the access time of the microprogram memory.

4. They occupy a large portion (typically 55%) of the CPU chip area.

(2) Hardwired control unit

A hardwired control unit is essentially a logic block, consisting of gates; flip-flops; decoders; and other digital circuits. When an instruction is read into the IR, the bit pattern, in combination with the bit pattern of the *sequence counter*, provides an input to the logic block, as shown in figure 9.4. The key fields in the instruction always line up with fixed input positions in the logic block; for example, the opcode bits might always line up with input positions 0 to 5. The output bit pattern provides control signals for the data path together with information needed to control the timing signal generated by the sequence counter on the next clock cycle. In this way each instruction causes an appropriate sequence of control signals to be generated. As with the microprogrammed control unit, condition codes or other information received from the data path can be used to alter the sequence of control signals.

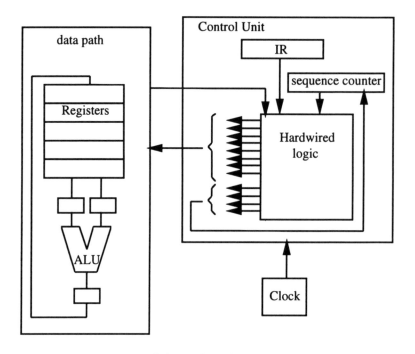

Figure 9.4 Hardwired control unit

Hardwired control units can only be altered by rearranging the wiring used to connect the various logic components together. This is a time consuming exercise and usually involves re-designing the complete logic block. On the other hand, hardwired control units are faster than their microprogrammed counterparts. This is because they avoid microprogram memory read operations, which tend to be slower than the basic Boolean operations performed by the hardwired decoder logic, and because they are optimised to take advantage of the regular instruction format.

The main points to noted about hardwired control units are:

1. They minimise the average number of clock cycles needed per instruction.

2. They occupy a relatively small area (typically 10%) of the CPU chip area.

3. They are less flexible than microprogrammed control units and cannot be easily modified without extensive re-design.

4. They are impractical for use with complex instruction formats.

9.5 Pipelining

Pipelining is the key implementation technique used to make faster CPUs and is extensively used in RISC processors. RISC processors allow instructions to be executed in stages, the stages being implemented using separate hardware. The stages are connected together to form an *instruction pipeline*, which allows more than one instruction to be processed at the same time. *Arithmetic pipelining* uses the same technique, allowing the operation to be broken down into smaller stages and implementing each stage with separate hardware. In this chapter, we will only consider instruction pipelining.

An instruction pipeline is like an assembly line, each stage being used to complete part of the instruction before passing it on to the next stage. In a typical pipelined RISC design, each instruction takes 1 clock cycle per stage, allowing the processor to accept a new instruction into the pipe after each clock cycle. Although this does not significantly alter the *latency* or number of cycles needed to complete an instruction, it does improve the overall throughput, one instruction completing per clock cycle. The operation of a typical four-stage or *depth 4* instruction pipeline is illustrated in figure 9.5.

Cycle	Stages			
	Fetch	Decode	Execute	Write-Back
1	inst 1			
2	inst 2	inst 1		
3	inst 3	inst 2	inst 1	
4	inst 4	inst 3	inst 2	inst 1
5	inst 5	inst 4	inst 3	inst 2

Figure 9.5 A four-stage instruction pipeline

The instruction fetch stage (IF) is used to fetch instructions from memory or an instruction cache into the first stage of the pipe. This requires the use of a *fetch unit*, which controls the Program Counter and buses to gain access to memory.

The instruction decode stage (ID) uses the control unit to decode the instruction and identify any source operands. Immediate operands and operands stored in the *register file* are moved into temporary ALU registers during this stage.

The execution stage (EX) is the stage in which the ALU performs operations on the operands stored in its temporary input registers and stores the result in its temporary output register.

The write-back stage (WB) is used to copy back the contents of the ALU's temporary output register to the register file.

The first instruction (inst 1) enters the pipeline during the first clock cycle and is followed on subsequent cycles by instructions 2, 3, 4 and so on. At the end of each clock cycle, an instruction is latched into the next stage, so that after 4 clock cycles, the first instruction completes. It is at this point that the power of pipelining starts to become apparent, because after the 5th clock cycle, the second instruction completes, after the 6th clock cycle, the third instruction and so on. In other words, after the pipe has been *filled*, one instruction is completed every clock cycle, giving a speedup factor of 4.

TQ 9.5   How did we arrive at a speedup factor of 4?

An important point to note in arriving at this figure is that we have ignored the latency caused by filling up the pipe. This reduces the speedup factor to a value less than four, as the following analysis shows.

If a k-stage pipeline executes (n) instructions using a clock with a cycle time (t), then without instruction overlap, the total time to execute the instructions would be:

$$T_S = nkt$$

If we now allow the instructions to be executed in parallel, by overlapping their stages of execution, then the time taken is:

$$T_P = kt + (n - 1)t$$

where kt, is the time for the pipe to fill up to the point where the first instruction completes and $(n - 1)t$ is the time taken for the remaining $(n - 1)$, instructions to execute at a rate of one per cycle. The speedup factor, S, is therefore:

$$S = \frac{nkt}{kt + (n - 1)t} = \frac{nk}{k + n - 1}$$

TQ 9.6   What is the speedup factor for a 4-stage pipeline when $n = 50$?

This last example shows that the speedup factor approaches the ideal value of 4, with long sequences of sequential instructions. Unfortunately, because of branch and other instructions that alter program flow, the pipeline sometimes becomes filled with instructions that are not needed. In such cases these instructions must be *flushed* from the pipe, so that the pipe can be filled with a new *stream* of instructions from the target address.

As we have seen, filling the pipe produces no throughput and wastes valuable clock cycles. Unless steps are taken to avoid this disruption, the performance advantages of using a pipeline can be severely reduced.

TQ 9.7   The MIPS R3000 uses a deeper 5-stage pipeline than the 4-stage pipeline used by SPARC processors. What disadvantage might there be in doing this?

Pipeline disruption can also be caused by instructions that need more than 1 clock cycle to execute, such as load instructions, or instructions that cannot proceed because they depend on the outcome of an earlier instruction that has not completed. Under such circumstances the pipeline may be forced to stop or *stall* for one or more clock cycles. The various sources of pipeline disruption are called *hazards*.

(1) Resource hazards

Main memory; caches; buses; register files; and functional units such as the ALU, are examples of some of the *resources* that must be shared by the instructions in a pipelined processor. If two stages need to access the same resource at any one time, then the pipeline must stall until the conflict is overcome. This can arise, for example, when a load instruction is being executed, because it needs to make use of the fetch unit also needed by the IF-stage to fetch another instruction into the pipe. Under such circumstances, the IF-stage must be delayed by one or more clock cycles until the operand has been moved into the register file, which effectively increases the average number of clock cycles per instruction.

The problems of resource hazards are generally overcome using hardware duplication. For example, the R3000 includes a separate Instruction and Data Cache while some implementations of the SPARC architecture use a dual instruction buffer for multiple instruction fetching.

Worked Example
Even with hardware duplication, if the instruction following a load instruction needs to access the operand being loaded, then a delay will occur. By referring to figure 9.5, explain why this is so.

Solution
After the load instruction is *issued* (moved from ID to EX stage), the following instruction, which is now in the ID stage, cannot be allowed to *read* the operand

and move it into temporary ALU registers until the load instruction has finished *writing* the operand into the register file.

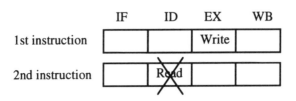

This is an example of a data hazard or a data dependency.

---

(2) Data hazards

The hazard identified in the previous example is a *read-after-write* hazard, because if the instruction following a load is allowed to read an operand from a register before a write operation has completed, then the program will fail to work properly. There are also two other types of data hazard: *write-after-read*, when an instruction attempts to write to a register before another instruction has finished reading it and *write-after-write*, when an instruction manages to write to a register before an earlier instruction has written to it.

TQ 9.8   Is it possible to have a read-after-read hazard?

Data hazards can be avoided by using a software approach that involves the compiler, or by using additional hardware.

Software approach

This approach relies on the compiler to identify and avoid data hazards, by rearranging the order in which the instructions are executed. For example, the following code contains a number of data dependencies.

```
lb      R2, A        ; load the byte at address A into register R2
addi    R3, R2, #7   ; put the sum of R2 and literal 7 into register R3
sb      R3, B        ; store the low-byte from R3 at address B
sub     R6, R4, R5   ; put the difference of R4 and R5 into register R6
```

When this code is compiled, a number of nop (no operation) instructions or *delay slots* are inserted between instructions that have data dependencies. This removes the dependencies but reduces the efficiency of the pipeline.

```
lb        R2, A
nop
addi      R3, R2, #7
nop
sb        R3, B
sub       R6, R4, R5
```

The compiler then attempts to fill the delay slots by re-scheduling the code, as shown below. For example, sub R6,R4,R5 can be moved into the first delay slot, because it does not depend upon register R2 and its repositioning does not affect the logical execution of the program.

```
lb        R2, A
sub       R6, R4, R5
addi      R3, R2, #7
nop
sb        R3, B
```

In practice about 70% of the delay slots can be filled in this way with a good compiler. This technique is sometimes referred to as *static scheduling*, because the program instructions are rearranged at compile time rather than at run time.

TQ 9.9   Would scheduling the code in this way affect program debugging?

Hardware approach

There are various hardware techniques that can be used to deal with data dependencies as they occur in the instruction stream, collectively called *dynamic scheduling*.

Figure 9.6(a) illustrates a read-before-write dependency, which arises when an instruction in the ID-stage attempts to use an operand from the register file, before it has been written back by an instruction currently in its EX-stage. It is not until this latter instruction completes the WB-stage, that valid data becomes available. To avoid stalling the pipeline, some architectures provide an additional data path to allow the operand from an instruction in the EX-stage to be forwarded directly from the ALU's temporary output register to one of its input registers, as shown in figure 9.6(b). This technique is called *operand forwarding* and requires hardware capable of dynamically detecting the data dependency and switching the output to the appropriate path.

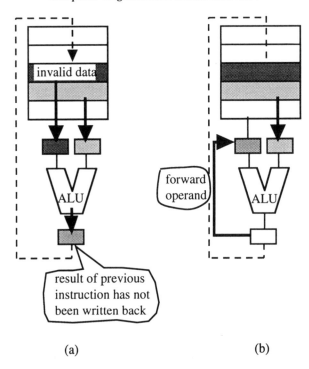

invalid data

ALU

forward
operand

ALU

result of previous
instruction has not
been written back

(a)　　　　　　　　　　　(b)

Figure 9.6 (a) Data dependency problem (b) Operand forwarding

Unfortunately, operand forwarding cannot overcome the problem of load/store instructions, which we described earlier. For short pipelines, load instructions are often dealt with by using a *hardware interlock* that detects the hazard and stalls the pipeline, following the *issue* of a load instruction from the ID-stage to the EX-stage. This remains in force until the load instruction has cleared the pipeline, which creates a delay or *bubble* in the pipe and increases the average number of Clock cycles Per Instruction (CPI). Only a few comparators are required to enforce the condition that all instructions following a load must be delayed, when the instruction immediately following it needs to access the operand being loaded.

The problem with *delayed loads* is that all instructions are held up just because one instruction depends on the outcome of the load operation. For pipelines with multiple execution units, it is possible to reduce the effect of this delay through a technique called *scoreboarding*. A simple form of scoreboarding is illustrated in figure 9.7.

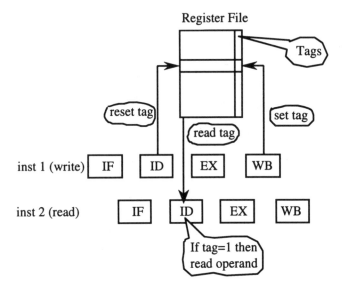

Figure 9.7 Simple scoreboarding technique

A 1-bit tag is included in the register file to indicate when a register contains valid data (tag = 1) or when the data is invalid (tag = 0). If an instruction is fetched that will write to a register, then during the ID-stage the tag associated with the register is reset (tag = 0). This indicates to any other instructions wishing to read the register that the value will be changed, and forces these instructions to wait. When the WB-stage is reached and the write instruction updates the register, the tag is automatically set (tag = 1), allowing any stalled instructions to proceed. The Motorola 88010 uses score-boarding to share its register file.

(3) Control hazards

Instructions that alter the Program Counter (PC) and hence the order in which instructions are executed, can also reduce pipeline performance. Such instructions include *branch* instructions, which can be either *conditional* or *unconditional*. Conditional branches generally pose more of a problem, as shown in figure 9.8.

After the pipe has been filled with the sequential instructions i, (i + 1), (i + 2), ..., etc. and (i + 1) reaches its WB-stage, the conditional branch instruction (i + 2) enters the EX-stage. At this point the outcome as to whether the branch is taken or not is resolved. As we will assume the branch is taken in this case, the instructions (i + 3) and (i + 4) are redundant and must be flushed out of the pipe before the correct instruction sequence j, (j + 1), (j + 2), ..., etc. can proceed. With this particular pipe, two clock cycles are wasted, which we call the *branch penalty*. Of course, if the branch is not taken then no penalty is incurred.

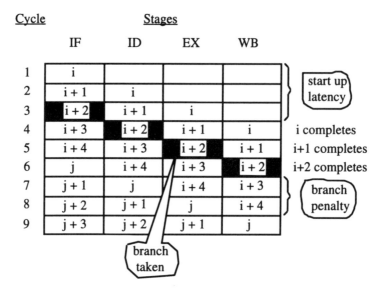

Figure 9.8 Effect of conditional branch instruction (i + 2)

TQ 9.10   Why would you expect an unconditional branch to incur a smaller
          branch penalty?

Because the probability of a branch instruction is quite high (typically between
10% and 30%), the effect of branch penalties can be very significant, especially if
the probability of the branch actually being taken is also high. In fact, if we
assume that:

   p_b = probability that an instruction is a branch
   p_t = probability that a branch is taken
   b = branch penalty
   CPI_{av} = average number of Clock cycles Per Instruction

Then it can be shown that $CPI_{av} = 1 + b.p_b.p_t$ [see Exercise 8]

TQ 9.11   If b = 2, p_b = 20% and p_t = 65% then what is CPI_{av}?

We can think of the probability $p_b.p_t$, as the effective fraction of the branch
penalty incurred by the instructions. If we call this fraction p_e, then the object of
any technique used to reduce the performance penalty of a branch instruction is to
make $p_e \ll 1$. We will now discuss some of these techniques.

Branch prediction

Branch prediction uses some additional logic to guess the outcome of a branch before it is resolved at the EX-stage. One way in which this can be done is to examine the opcode at the decode stage and to make a presumption on the outcome, such as: 'all Branch on Equal instructions are taken' or 'Branch on Minus instructions are never taken'. The appropriate instructions are then fetched based on these premises, in the hope that they are correct, at least most of the time. Although this form of *static* branch prediction is relatively simple, it cannot be adapted to the particular instruction usage of a given program. With *dynamic* branch prediction however, account of program usage is taken using a small *branch history table*. This table is used to record the outcome of branch instructions that have already been executed and to predict the outcome of these instructions the next time they are executed. This is of special importance with program loops, where a branch might be executed several hundred times before an exit is made. Getting the prediction wrong every time, which could be the case with static prediction, would severely affect performance.

Branch bypassing

By using separate First-In-First-Out (FIFO) instruction buffers, it is possible to fetch both the instruction sequence following a branch and those from the branch target at the same time. This prevents the processor from stalling and allows it to continue processing instructions irrespective of whether the branch is taken, as illustrated in figure 9.9.

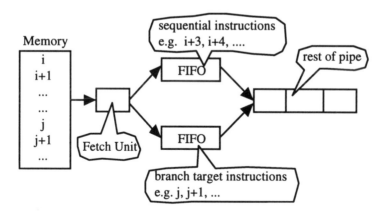

Figure 9.9 Dual-buffer branch bypass

The buffer containing the unused instruction is merely flushed, the next time a conditional branch is encountered in the instruction stream.

Unfortunately, if two or more conditional branch instructions manage to enter a buffer, then this technique breaks down. This can be overcome by using additional buffers, but this adds to the cost of the implementation.

Delayed branch

This is a software approach and uses static scheduling in the same way as it was used when we considered data dependency. At compile time, a number of delay slots are inserted after the conditional branch instructions, which the compiler tries to fill with instructions that will be executed whether the branch is taken or not. For example, the compiler can determine whether a few instructions which precede the branch can be moved into the delay slots after the branch. In this way, when the branch executes, these instructions are still executed and therefore there is no need to flush the buffer. As with delayed loads, the nop instructions used to create the delay slots cannot always be filled, so a certain percentage of branch penalty can still be expected.

9.6 Microprocessor Performance

When describing microprocessor performance we are primarily concerned with the time it takes the CPU to execute a program. This is the CPU time and is given by:

$$\text{CPU time} = \text{cycles for program (n)} \times \text{clock cycle time (T)}$$
$$= \text{CPI} \times \text{number of instructions (I)} \times \text{T}$$

where CPI is the average number of Clock cycles Per Instruction.

The shorter the CPU time, the better the performance (P), which we can express in terms of the instruction execution rate as:

$$P = \frac{1}{\text{CPU time}} = \frac{1}{\text{CPI} \times \text{I} \times \text{T}}$$

Because $\frac{1}{T}$ = the clock frequency (f), then $P = \dfrac{f}{\text{CPI} \times \text{I}}$

If f is expressed in MHz and I in millions of instructions, then P is in MIPS (Million Instructions Per Second).

TQ 9.12   What is the value of P for a SPARC processor that is clocked at 16.67 MHz, when it takes on average, 1.3 CPI to execute 1.2 million instructions?

Because different programs have different mixes of instructions, the value of P varies according to the type of program under test. For this reason, when comparing processor performance, synthetic programs or *benchmarks* are often used. These have a representative mix of the types of instruction used in real programs.

9.7 Superscalar and Superpipelined Architectures

Pipelines are also included on a number of CISC processors, such as the MC68040 and Intel 80486. Unfortunately, much of the software written for these CISC processors was not produced with 'pipeline-aware' compilers and therefore, unlike RISC processors, they cannot always take full advantage of the potential speedup offered. As VLSI technology has evolved, the basic pipeline structure we have described so far has been extended in an attempt to increase instruction overlap.

With *superpipelining*, instruction execution is broken down into even finer steps by lengthening the pipeline to increase *granularity*. For example, the R4000 uses a superpipelined 8-stage instruction pipeline that is able to deliver 50 MIPS at 50 MHz, compared with only 20 MIPS at 25 MHz offered by its non-superpipelined predecessor, the R3000. The increased performance arises because each stage can execute in under half a clock cycle. By doubling the internal clock speed, two stages and hence two instructions can be completed in one external clock cycle. In the case of the R4300, an on-chip frequency divide circuit is used to clock the pipeline at 100 MHz from an external 50 MHz clock source. One drawback of these long pipelines is that they are more susceptible to data dependency and require more 'intelligent' compilers.

An alternative way of increasing internal parallelism is to allow multiple instructions to be issued in the same clock cycle. This requires the duplication of various pipeline stages and the inclusion of multiple execution units, so that for example, an instruction requiring a floating point add operation can be executed concurrently with one requiring an integer arithmetic operation. Processors that support this type of architecture are called multiple-issue processors and there are two basic types: superscalar processors such as the Intel Pentium, that schedules parallel execution within variable length blocks of five or so instructions using static/dynamic scheduling; and Very Long Instruction Word (VLIW) processors which use static scheduling techniques to issue fixed size blocks of instructions or instruction words of between about 256 and 1024 bits, each field being used to encode an operation for a particular execution unit. Using sophisticated *trace scheduling* and other compilation techniques, these VLIW processors take advantage of program-wide parallelism amongst the instructions and are potentially much faster than superscalar processors. Their main drawback is that the compilers for these processors are slow and expensive and also the code is specifically targeted for a specific architecture and cannot be ported to a similar architecture unless the number of execution units and their respective latencies can be matched.

9.8 Summary

In this chapter we have described the main characteristics that distinguish RISC processors from conventional CISC processors. We explained the differences between their instruction sets and the control units used to decode their instructions. Because of the simplicity and regularity of the RISC instruction set, we explained how RISC designs used instruction pipelining to speed up the instruction execution rate. We then went on to discuss the resource, data and control hazards that could disrupt the pipeline and reduce its efficiency, together with some of the techniques currently used to overcome them. Throughout the chapter we emphasised the importance of RISC compilers for scheduling instructions and taking advantage of the underlying architecture. The chapter concluded with a brief description of superpiplined, superscalar and VLIW architectures.

9.9 Answers to Text Questions

TQ 9.1   You would probably expect RISC programs to be longer, because several simple instructions would be needed to do the same job as one complex instruction. This is called code expansion. However, thro-ugh the use of code size optimisation, RISC compilers can usually generate code that is at least within 15% and sometimes even shorter than the equivalent CISC code.

TQ 9.2   The 68000 has a number of variable-length formats and several instruction coding schemes.

TQ 9.3   The two operations [MBR] ← [M(MAR)], use 400 ns and therefore over half the instruction cycle is spent accessing memory.

TQ 9.4   Because the CWP only uses 5 bits.

TQ 9.5   If each instruction was completed before the next instruction started, then it would take 4 clock cycles per instruction. With our 4-stage pipeline, this is reduced to 1 clock cycle per instruction, so instructions appear to execute 4 times faster.

TQ 9.6 $\quad S = \dfrac{50 \times 4}{4 + 50 - 1} = 3.8$

TQ 9.7   If the pipe needs to be flushed, then it takes more clock cycles to refill the pipeline.

TQ 9.8   No, changing the order in which the two instructions read a register will not invalidate the operation of the program.

TQ 9.9   Yes, debugging a program by single stepping through the code would be more difficult to follow. In practice, debugging is normally carried out *before* optimising the code.

TQ 9.10   Because it can be detected at the ID-stage, which reduces the number of redundant instructions fetched into the pipe.

TQ 9.11 $CPI_{av} = 1 + 2 \times 0.2 \times 0.65 = 1.26$ rather than the ideal value of 1.

TQ 9.12 $\quad P = \dfrac{16.67}{1.3 \times 1.2} = 10.69$ MIPS

9.10 Exercises

1. List five important characteristics that could be used to distinguish RISC from CISC architectures. Why do RISC architectures tend to use large register files?

2. Describe how register windows are used with SPARC architectures to pass parameters between procedures. How does the R3000 deal with this problem?

3. Describe a typical operation performed by a microinstruction.
   List the advantages and disadvantages of a microprogrammed control unit compared with a hardwired control unit.

4. An n-stage instruction pipeline can potentially increase the instruction throughput by a factor of n. Why is this seldom the case in practice?

5. In what ways do RISC compilers differ from CISC compilers?

6. Using a suitable example, explain what is meant by data dependency. Describe a dynamic scheduling technique to overcome this.

7. Why do conditional branch instructions tend to reduce the efficiency of an instruction pipeline? Explain what is meant by a delayed branch.

8. Given the following information about a pipeline:

    p_b = probability that an instruction is a branch
    p_t = probability that a branch is taken
    b = branch penalty

    Then out of n instructions in a pipeline, how many will be

    (i)   branch instructions?
    (ii)   non-branch instructions?
    (iii) branch instructions which when resolved result in a branch being taken?
    (iv)   branch instructions which when resolved do not result in a branch being taken?

    If it takes $(1 + b)$ clock cycle to execute branch instructions that actually take place and only 1 clock cycle per instruction for the rest, then:

    (v)   How many clock cycles are needed to execute the n instructions?
    (vi)   What is the average number of clock cycles per instruction?

9. What is meant by a superscalar processor?
    A VLIW processor uses a 256-bit instruction word, each instruction being encoded using 32 bits. Estimate the processor's performance if it is clocked at 100 MHz.

References

Byte (1996), *The Word on VLIW,* McGraw-Hill, **21**, 4, Apr 96, pp. 61-64
Gorsline, G.W. (1986), *Computer Organisation,* Prentice Hall, pp. 307-308.
Heudin, J.C., Panetto, C. (1992), *RISC Architectures,* Chapman & Hall.
Klein, D.V.(1989), *RISC vs CISC from the Perspective of Compiler/ Instruction Set Interaction,* Proc. European UNIX Users Group, Vienna.
URL *http://infopad.eecs.berkelet.edu/CIC*
Wilkinson, B. (1991), *Computer Architecture,* Prentice Hall, pp. 144-167.

10 *Parallel Architectures*

In the previous chapter we described how pipelining and other forms of low-level parallelism could be used to enhance processor performance. Although such techniques can increase performance by a factor of 10 or so, uniprocessor systems continue to be limited by the rate at which instructions can be issued and operands supplied. As VLSI technology has reduced the size and cost of computer components, interconnecting several processors with several memory modules has offered designers the opportunity of building parallel systems with much greater performance characteristics than uniprocessor systems. These parallel architectures also tend to introduce some degree of fault-tolerance, so that if a component or interconnection fails, the system tends to degrade rather than stop. This chapter explores some of these architectures.

10.1 Classifying Parallel Architectures

There are several ways of classifying parallel architectures. In this section we will describe two of them.

(1) Flynn's classification scheme

Flynn classified computer architectures [Flynn 66] on the basis of how many *instruction streams* and how many operand or *data streams* they could handle simultaneously. He defined four classes:

1. SISD (Single Instruction Stream - Single Data Stream)

This class describes von Neumann style architectures, where a single set of instructions are fetched serially or sequentially and which act upon single data items.

2. MIMD (Multiple Instruction Stream - Multiple Data Stream)

This class describes multiprocessor systems, where at least two processors execute separate streams of instructions that act upon different data items.

3. SIMD (Single Instruction Stream - Multiple Data Stream)

This class includes systems such as array processors, in which a single stream of instructions is generated by a control processor and broadcast to a number of separate arithmetic processors. The arithmetic processors execute the same instruction in lockstep, using separate data items.

4. MISD (Multiple Instruction Stream - Single Data Stream)

This class was added for completeness rather than because there are any good representative examples of such architectures.

Unfortunately, this rather elegant classification scheme is now outdated and fails to take account of some of the more recent developments in parallel architectures.

(2) Duncan's classification scheme

Duncan's scheme [Duncan 90] was introduced in an attempt to include architectures that did not fit conveniently into Flynn's scheme and to exclude architectures that were basically serial, even though they used low-level parallel mechanisms. Duncan's scheme is illustrated in figure 10.1.

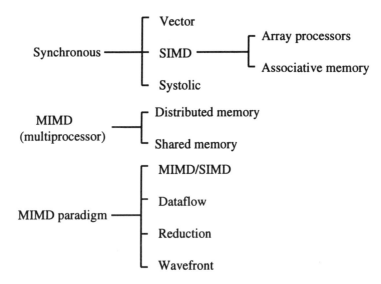

Figure 10.1 Duncan's classification scheme

The scheme continues to use some of Flynn's terminology, whilst making a distinction between architectures that perform parallel operations in *lockstep* (synchronous architectures), and those that operate asynchronously (MIMD architectures). In the following sections of this chapter, we will examine a small selection of these architectures.

10.2 SIMD Array Processors

An array processor performs computations on large arrays of data, frequently needed for large-scale scientific calculations such as image processing and nuclear energy modelling. The organisation of a typical SIMD array processor is shown in figure 10.2.

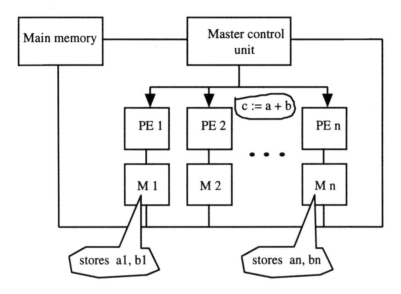

Figure 10.2 SIMD array processor organisation

The processor contains several identical *Processing Elements* (PEs), each having a local memory (M) in which operands are stored before and after a computation. The master control unit fetches instructions from main memory and decodes them. If they are vector instructions, it simultaneously broadcasts them to all the PE's. Each PE then performs the same computational operation in lockstep fashion on its local data. For example, to perform the vector addition $C := A + B$, where A and B are vectors $(a_1, a_2, ..., a_n)$ and $(b_1, b_2, ..., b_n)$ respectively, the control unit loads each memory module M_i with operands a_i and b_i and then broadcasts the instruction $c := a + b$.

For vectors shorter than n, there are various masking schemes that can be used to inhibit selected PEs from responding to the instruction. Also, the master control unit has sufficient processing capability to execute scalar and control instructions directly.

10.3 Dataflow Computers

Unlike von Neumann computers, which use a program counter (PC) to control the flow of instruction execution, *dataflow* or *data driven* computers have no PC and execute instructions as soon as their operands become available. Dataflow programs are represented by *data dependency graphs*. A program fragment to evaluate the expression $(3 * a + 4 * b)$, is illustrated in figure 10.3.

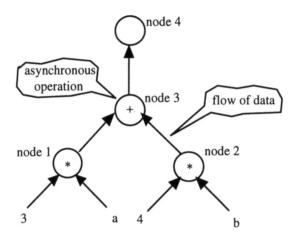

Figure 10.3 Data dependency graph of a program fragment

Each node operates independently, performing its particular operation or *firing* as soon as it has received all of its operands. The result operand is then passed onto the next node or nodes in the graph. The number of nodes that can be fired simultaneously depends upon the organisation of the hardware.

Figure 10.4 illustrates a ring structured implementation of a dataflow computer. Tokens are used to represent operands and instructions, which are passed between the functional units in pipeline fashion. In the figure, we have included some of the tokens that are created as the program fragment illustrated in figure 10.3 is executed.

Stage-1 represents the point just after node 2 has fired, when a *data token* has been created and entered into the FIFO token queue. The data token contains the result of the multiplication operation and its destination node, node 3. In this example we have assumed that the token has a value of 3.

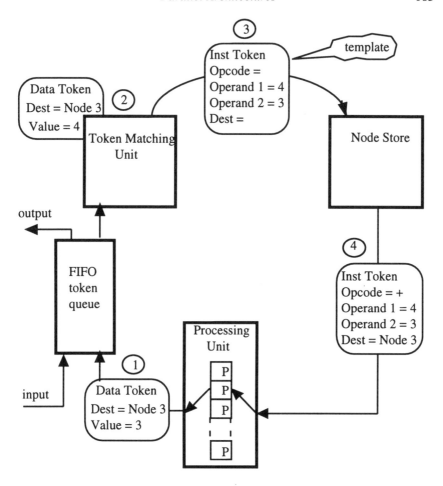

Figure 10.4 Ring structured dataflow organisation

In Stage-2, the data token is passed into the token matching unit, where an associative search takes place to find any other operands required by the instruction at node 3. Because the token associated with the firing of node 1 has already been created and stored there, a match takes place and an instruction token *template* is created.

In Stage-3, the Node Store is used to fill in the relevant token fields in the template, such as the opcode and the destination node.

Finally in Stage-4, the executable token is passed to the processing unit where one of the available processors is used to execute the instruction, '+' , on the operands 3 and 4. The operation results in the creation of a new data token.

TQ 10.1   Describe the data token created.

The FIFO token buffer, which also acts as an IO interface, is used to pass the final result of the computation out of the system.

10.4 MIMD Systems

General purpose MIMD multiprocessor systems have a number of independent processors that operate upon separate data streams using separate instruction streams. In this section we describe two different architectural models: one is *tightly-coupled*, in which multiprocessors access instructions and data through a globally shared main memory, and the other is *loosely-coupled*, where each processor has a large local memory which it can use to access most of its instructions and data. After considering the advantages and disadvantages of these models, we will briefly discuss the distributed shared memory approach to multiprocessor systems.

(1) Shared memory MIMD systems

Figure 10.5 is a generic model of a shared memory MIMD system. Processors P_1, P_2, ... , P_n communicate and handle data processing tasks by accessing a shared memory. Because any processor can handle any task such systems are also referred to as *symmetric multiprocessor* systems.

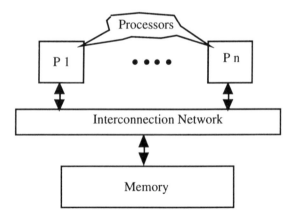

Figure 10.5 Model of a shared memory MIMD system

There are a variety of interconnection networks that can be used and a number of techniques to ensure mutual exclusion. One of the simplest and most widespread methods of interconnecting the processors is through a time-shared bus.

Time-shared bus

The general organisation of a *time-shared bus* system is shown in figure 10.6, where we have assumed that each processor has a separate local cache memory for storing instructions and data. The single shared bus is used to allow processors $P_1,...,P_n$ to gain access to memory and input/output devices.

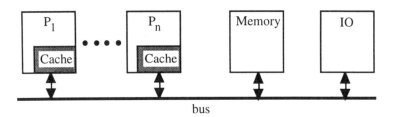

Figure 10.6 Shared memory architecture using a time-shared bus

When a processor wishes to access memory, it must first check whether the bus is available before taking control of the bus and proceeding with the transfer. While one processor is using the bus, others can only access their local cache and must wait for the processor to relinquish control of the bus before they can access the shared memory. The shared bus is therefore a source of contention. If simultaneous requests are made for the bus, including requests by IO controllers (see §7.5), then some form of arbitration must take place to decide which processor can proceed and which must wait. This can be done by assigning different priorities to the processors using a hardware device called a *bus arbiter*.

One of the major problems with sharing a common bus is bus saturation, which arises when too many processors are connected. Under such circumstances, processors spend most of their time waiting to become bus master, rather than executing instructions. This bottleneck is partially alleviated by providing each processor with a local cache, but unfortunately this introduces another problem called *multi-cache coherency*.

With multiple cache memories, several copies of the same data can exist throughout the system. If one processor updates its cache, for example by performing a write-through operation (see §6.5), then 'stale' data is left in all other local caches that have accessed the same block. To prevent this from disrupting the program, some form of *dynamic coherency checking* is needed to invalidate these cache entries and possibly update them with 'valid' data. One popular way of doing this is to use a coherency protocol called *snooping*.

With snooping, all cache controllers monitor or *snoop* the bus to determine whether or not they have a copy of the shared block. When a *write-invalidate* protocol is used, the processor wishing to update its local cache issues an invalidation signal over the bus before doing so. All controllers receive this signal and check to see if they have a copy of the block; if so, they invalidate their copy of the block by setting an invalid bit in the cache line. An alternative snooping protocol is *write-update*, where the processor wishing to update its cache broadcasts the new data over the bus, which allows the other caches to update their entries rather than invalidate them.

When it comes to reading, a processor checks its local cache in the usual way. If a 'miss' occurs, then if a write-back policy is used, all other local caches must check to see if they have a copy of the requested data. If they do, then this data must be supplied to the requesting processor; otherwise it must be fetched from the shared memory.

TQ 10.2   Why is a write-back and not a write-through policy preferred in a
          shared bus multiprocessor system?

Crossbar switch

Another way of interconnecting processors with a shared memory is to use a number of memory modules and to connect the processors to these module using an array of switches. This type of interconnection network is called a *crossbar switch* as shown in figure 10.7.

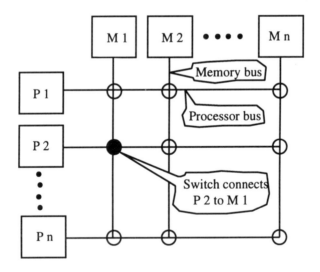

Figure 10.7 Shared memory architecture using an n × n crossbar switch

Switches are complex devices capable of connecting a processor's data, address and control bus to one of the memory modules. Each switch contains arbitration logic to resolve multiple requests for access to the same module.

The main advantage in using a crossbar switch is that the problem of bus contention we found with a shared bus is now reduced to the occasional contention for a memory bus. Other than this, processors can proceed to access memory modules in parallel, which significantly increases the data transfer rate.

Another advantage of this interconnection topology is that it allows the network to be reconfigured dynamically. Its disadvantage arises from the cost of the hardware and the fact that the number of switches increases as the square of the number of processors. For this reason, crossbar-switched networks only tend to be used for connecting a small number of processors.

Multiport memory

A crossbar switch prevents two processors from accessing the same memory module, even when different locations within the module are involved. Multiport memories overcome this by incorporating device switching in the module itself.

The memory module contains a number of ports, each port being used to connect a separate processor through a dedicated bus, as shown in figure 10.8.

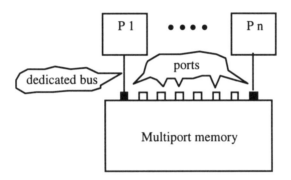

Figure 10.8 Shared memory architecture using a multiport memory

Arbitration logic is included to prevent more than one processor from accessing the same memory location at any one time, with different priority levels being assigned to each port.

One advantage in using multiport memories is that it is possible to include memory protection, by designating portions of memory as private to certain processors. One drawback in doing this is that it reduces the *fault tolerance* of the system.

As with crossbar switches, multiport memories are expensive and it is therefore difficult to justify their use in systems that use a large number of processors.

TQ 10.3   Why does the use of designated portions of private memory reduce the fault tolerance of the system?

Scaling shared memory systems

Shared memory architectures are limited in the number of processors that can be connected to memory. This is because as we try to increase throughput by adding more processors, we increase memory contention, which in turn reduces performance. Beyond a certain break-even point, little advantage is gained in scaling the system any further, as illustrated in figure 10.9.

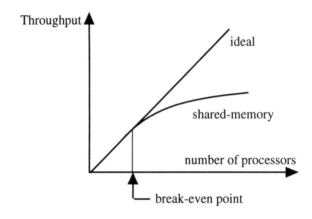

Figure 10.9 Effect of scaling on throughput for a shared memory system

Although techniques such as crossbar switching and multiport memories can reduce this problem, the cost of the system tends to scale disproportionately with the number of processors, making large multiprocessor systems unattractive.

(2) Distributed memory MIMD systems

Unlike shared memory systems, distributed memory MIMD or *multicomputer systems* offer the potential of linear scalability, because each processor has its own local memory and processors do not share variables. Instead, processors exchange data by sending messages to each other across some form of communication network. The basic organisation of a distributed memory MIMD system is shown in figure 10.10.

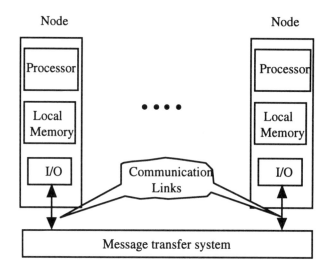

Figure 10.10 Model of a distributed memory MIMD system

Each node contains a processor, some local memory and a number of communication links for exchanging messages through the message transfer system. Although conventional processors can be used, the task of preparing and sending a message across the network tends to be notoriously slow and this leads to an excessive communication overhead. This is due to the fact that message-passing is carried out using software and there are no in-built facilities for handling messages. When specialised message-passing processors are used, this overhead can be significantly reduced.

Transputer

The INMOS transputer family [Inmos 88] was specifically designed for building message-passing multiprocessor systems. Each transputer includes on a single VLSI chip: a processor; some local memory; and in the case of the T414, four high-speed (20 Mbps) full-duplex bit-serial communication links, as shown in figure 10.11.

The T414 has a 32-bit RISC architecture with 2 kbytes of on-chip RAM and a memory interface capable of addressing 4 Gbytes of external memory. The point-to-point links operate autonomously, allowing message-passing to be overlapped with instruction processing.

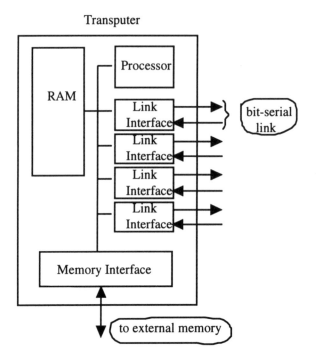

Figure 10.11 Conceptual organisation of a transputer

Each transputer can execute one or more processes. Processes communicate through *channels*, each channel being an abstract connection between exactly two processes. If processes reside on the same transputer, channels are implemented using memory words and if they exists on separate transputers, channels are implemented using serial links.

When two processes exchange data, one process writes bytes to a channel while the other reads and stores them in its local memory. If a process tries to send or receive data through a channel before a second process is ready to read it, the transputer automatically deschedules the sending process until the receiver process is ready. Likewise, if a receiver process becomes ready before a sender process, it too is descheduled until the sender is ready. This *synchronisation* between processes is performed automatically in hardware.

If processes reside on non-adjacent transputers, messages must be routed through one or more intermediate nodes. These nodes must be programmed to perform this routing function.

With four links, several interconnection topologies are possible, as illustrated in figure 10.12. The topology is normally chosen to reflect certain features of the computation and to reduce the latency caused by message-passing across the network.

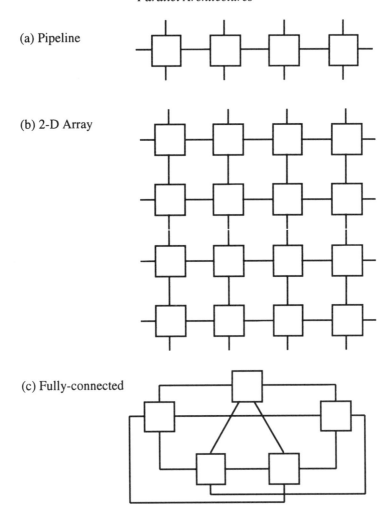

(a) Pipeline

(b) 2-D Array

(c) Fully-connected

Figure 10.12 Transputer interconnection topologies

The pipeline topology is often used because several different types of algorithm can be adapted to this arrangement. One of the main disadvantages with this configuration is the fact that, for an n-node pipeline, 2n links remain unused. Potentially these could be used for reducing the message-passing overhead.

Two-dimensional (2-D) arrays are widely used for algorithms with predominantly local communication patterns such as image processing applications. Using an n-node array of transputers for non-local communication can lead to severe degradation due to the fact that some messages may have to traverse as many as $2(\sqrt{n} - 1)$ links. Communication kernels based on message routing or packet switching techniques have been developed for more general communication, but at the expense of reduced bandwidth and increased message-passing latency.

The fully-connected network overcomes the communication   problems between processes on separate nodes, but with only four links the maximum number of nodes in such a network is limited to five.

TQ 10.4   Estimate the average number of links traversed by a message in a 2-D
          array of 16 transputers.

Hypercube

Currently, the best solution to the problem of scaling a distributed memory system, without unduly increasing the average message-passing latency, is the *hypercube*. With a hypercube topology, N processors are arranged in a k-dimensional cube, where $N = 2^k$. Examples of these topologies are shown in figure 10.13.

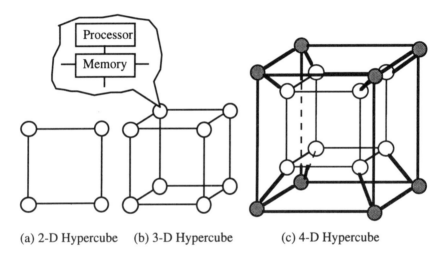

(a) 2-D Hypercube   (b) 3-D Hypercube   (c) 4-D Hypercube

Figure 10.13 Examples of hypercube topologies

Each node contains a processor, a local memory and a number of communication links. Unlike the transputer, the number of links per node varies according to the dimension used. It can be shown that an n-node hypercube reduces the maximum message path length to ($\log_2 n$).

TQ 10.5   Estimate the average path length traversed by a message in a 16-node
          hypercube.

---

(3) Distributed shared memory systems

Distributed shared memory (DSM) systems provide a virtual shared memory abstraction on top of a message-passing distributed memory system. This allows code based on a shared memory model, such as C and FORTRAN, to be ported and compiled with a good chance of parallel speedup, whilst continuing to take advantage of the scalability offered by a distributed memory organisation. Figure 10.14 gives a conceptual view of a DSM system.

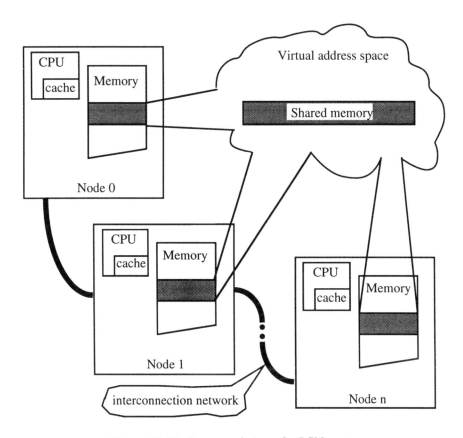

Figure 10.14 Conceptual view of a DSM system

The computational nodes are tied together by a ring or other interconnection network, each node consisting of one or more CPUs connected to a local mem-ory through a time-shared bus, crossbar switch or other local network. Data is shared amongst the nodes and virtual addresses generated by the CPUs (see §8.7) are translated by hardware/software into the physical addresses needed to locate the data. When data is held locally, it is returned across the local network in the usual way. If however the data is held off-node, then the virtual address must be converted into a message that is sent across the interconnection network to a distant node.

The way the shared data is distributed among the nodes (*structure*) and the unit of sharing used (*granularity*) are closely related and depend upon the way the DSM system is implemented. For example, if it is implemented using an extended form of caching, then the unit of sharing is usually the size of a cache line, while if it is implemented using virtual memory management hardware, then pages are normally exchanged. Whether this data is 'owned' by a node or allowed to migrate freely from one node to another (*dynamic redistribution*), also depends upon the implementation and this in turn affects the technique used to locate and access the data. Also, since most DSM systems replicate data in an effort to allow parallel data accesses, then support for memory coherency must be provided using some form of coherence protocol.

As research into these and other issues continues, DSM systems promise to be an effective way of enabling users to gracefully migrate towards parallel processing.

10.5 Amdahl's Law

One of the reasons for using a parallel architecture is to increase the speed at which a computational task can be undertaken. We can define the speedup S, gained by using a multiprocessor platform of (n) processors to be:

$$S(n) = \frac{\text{Time to execute task on a uniprocessor system}}{\text{Time to execute task on a multiprocessor system}}$$

Ideally, S is a linear function of n, but in practice this is rarely the case. This is because, in addition to delays caused by memory contention and message-passing latency, the computational task usually contains a proportion of sequential instructions that cannot take advantage of any additional processing power. In 1967 an argument put forth by Gene Amdahl [Amdahl 67] showed that even with a very large number of processors, the maximum speedup obtainable is dominated by the fraction of serial work in any given problem. The argument goes as follows:

Consider a computational task being carried out using (n) processors. If (s) is the amount of time spent by a processor on serial parts of the program and (p) is the amount of time spent on parts of the program that can be split amongst the n processors and done in parallel, then Amdahl's law says that the speedup (S) is given as:

$$S = (s + p) / (s + p/n)$$

TQ 10.6   If s = 10s and p = 90s, then what speedup would we expect to gain with
9 processors?

If we make (s + p) = 1, then s and p become fractions of the total time required
to perform the computation on a uniprocessor system. We can then set p = (1 − s)
to give:

$$S = 1 / (s + (1 - s)/n) = n / ((n - 1)s + 1)$$

A graph of this relationship is given in figure 10.15.

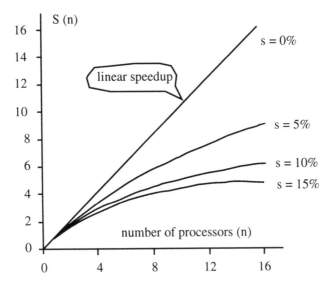

Figure 10.15 Speedup versus processors

From this graph we can see that the speedup is dominated by the fraction of
the computation that must be executed serially. For example, with s = 10% and n
= 16, we get a speedup of about 6 and not 16 as one might expect. Also we can
see that there is little to be gained by increasing the number of processors beyond
about 12. Only when s is very small, can the cost of adding additional processors
to the system be justified in terms of throughput.

TQ 10.7   For a given problem how might we go about reducing the value of s?

10.6 Summary

In this chapter we described a number of parallel architectures and introduced two different schemes for classifying them. After introducing the array processor (SIMD) and the dataflow computer (MIMD-paradigm), we concentrated upon general purpose MIMD systems. These included shared memory and distributed memory systems. We described how a time-shared bus, a crossbar switch and multiport memory could be used to allow several processors to share access to a memory. We then explained how memory contention tended to degrade these systems when they were scaled up by adding more processors. Then we described how distributed memory systems avoided this problem by passing data via messages and introduced the transputer as an example of a message-passing processor. After describing some of the different topologies that could be constructed with transputers we introduced the hypercube and explained how it reduced message-passing latency. We then briefly touched on distributed shared memory (DSM) systems as a compromise between the scalability of distributed memory and the ease of programming offered by shared memory systems. Finally, we discussed Amdahl's Law and showed how the sequential fraction of a computation could radically alter the speedup factor of a parallel system.

10.7 Answers to Text Questions

TQ 10.1   The data token contains the destination node, node 4, and the data value 7.

TQ 10.2   Because it reduces the amount of bus traffic and allows more processors on a single bus.

TQ 10.3   If a processor develops a fault, then other processors may be unable to access information needed for the system to continue operating.

TQ 10.4   Since the maximum number of links traversed is $2(\tilde{A}16 - 1)$ then the average is $\dfrac{6}{2} = 3$.

TQ 10.5   Average path length is $(\log_2 16) / 2 = 2$.

TQ 10.6 $S = (10 + 90)/(10 + 90/9) = 100/20 = 5$.

TQ 10.7   We might consider using different parallel algorithms.

10.8 Exercises

1. Give two reasons why multiprocessor systems are useful.

2. What do you understand by the terms, *instruction stream* and *data stream*? Explain how Flynn uses the stream concept to classify multiprocessor systems.

3. What is the main difference between a control-flow processor and a data-driven processor? Draw a data dependency graph to represent the following computation: a * (b + c) – d.

4. Describe two ways of implementing an interconnection network in a shared memory multiprocessor system. State one advantage and one disadvantage of each organisation.

5. With shared memory multiprocessor systems, the processors are often equipped with cache memories. Explain how these caches reduce the problem of memory contention and what steps must be taken to ensure cache coherency.

6. What do you understand by the term *scalability*, when describing a multiprocessor system? Why are tightly-coupled systems more difficult to scale than loosely-coupled systems?

7. One of the problems with a large array of transputers is that processors near the centre tend to become saturated. Why is this and what steps might be taken to alleviate the problem?

8. How many nodes are there in a four-dimensional hypercube? Estimate the average path length traversed by a typical message and compare your answer with that produced by a 2D-array of transputers having the same number of nodes.

9. What do you understand by the terms *granularity* and *memory-coherency* when discussing a DSM system? On some systems, a node makes a request for data by broadcasting it to all other nodes, while on others, a centralised server is used to keep track of all shared data. Discuss the advantages and disadvantages of these techniques in terms of access time, load balancing and scalability.

10. Estimate the speedup you might expect to gain in using a parallel processing platform with 16 processors, if only 75% of a computational task can be divided into processes that can be executed in parallel. State any assumptions made.

References

Amdahl, G.M. (1967), *Validity of the single-processor approach to achieving large scale computing capabilities*, Proc. AFIPS, **30**, pp. 483-485.

Amza, C. *et al* (1996), *TreadMarks: Shared Memory Computing on Networks of Workstations,* Computer, **29**, 2, Feb 96, pp. 18-28

Duncan, R. (1990), *A Survey of Parallel Computer Architectures*, Computer, **23**, 2, Feb 90.

Flynn, M.J. (1966), *Very High-Speed Computing Systems*, Proc. IEEE, **54**,12, Dec 66.

Harp, R.G. (1989), *Transputer Applications*, UCL Press, London.

Ibbett, R.N., Topham, N.P. (1989), *Architecture of High Performance Computers Vol II*, Macmillan Press, London. pp. 141-167

INMOS Ltd (1988), *The transputer reference manual*, Prentice Hall, New Jersey.

Lilja, D.J. (1991), *Architectural Alternatives For Exploiting Parallelism*, IEEE Computer Society Press, California, pp. 354-362

Appendix 1 - ASCII Table

b3	b2	b1	b0	b6	0	0	0	0	1	1	1	1
				b5	0	0	1	1	0	0	1	1
				b4	0	1	0	1	0	1	0	1
0	0	0	0		NL	DLE	SP	0	@	P		p
0	0	0	1		SOH	DC1	!	1	A	Q	a	q
0	0	1	0		STX	DC2	"	2	B	R	b	r
0	0	1	1		ETX	DC3	=	3	C	S	c	s
0	1	0	0		EOT	DC4	$	4	D	T	d	t
0	1	0	1		ENQ	NAK	%	5	E	U	e	u
0	1	1	0		ACK	SYN	&	6	F	V	f	v
0	1	1	1		BEL	ETB	'	7	G	W	g	w
1	0	0	0		BS	CAN	(	8	H	X	h	x
1	0	0	1		HT	EM	)	9	I	Y	i	y
1	0	1	0		LF	SUB	*	:	J	Z	j	z
1	0	1	1		VT	ESC	+	;	K	[	k	{
1	1	0	0		FF	FS	,	<	L	\	l	|
1	1	0	1		CR	GS	-	=	M	]	m	}
1	1	1	0		SO	RS	.	>	N	^	n	~
1	1	1	1		SI	US	/	?	O	_	o	DEL

$b_6, b_5, ..., b_0$ are the seven bit positions, numbered from left to right.

Appendix 2 - Answers to Exercises

This appendix contains brief answers to selected exercises in the book.

Chapter 1

3. ROM is needed for storing programs and data that needs to be available when the computer is first switched on.

5. (a) Control Unit (b) Arithmetic and Logic Unit.

8. The program needs to be recompiled in order to produce the machine instructions that can be 'understood' by the processor in the new machine.

Chapter 2

1.

A	x
0	1
1	0

(a)

A	B	x
0	0	1
0	1	1
1	0	1
1	1	0

(b)

For the first circuit, a NOT gate would perform the same function, and for the second circuit, a NAND gate could be used.

4.

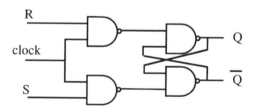

6.

clock transition	Q2	Q1	Q0
0	1	1	1
1	1	1	0
2	1	0	1
3	1	0	0
4	0	1	1
5	0	1	0
6	0	0	1
7	0	0	0

Chapter 3

2. (a) 10000 (b) 01111111 (c) 11111111

4. (a) AEB (b) E6 (c) 0A3

6. 8K

8.

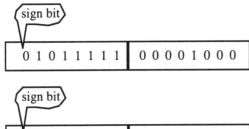

Chapter 4

4. This would cause a jump or branch to another part of the program.

5. This is because the processor fetches two bytes at a time.

Chapter 5

1. (a) 0011 0110 0000 0111 (b) 0111 1100 0000 0101

3. (a)   SWAP   D0
                    MOVE.B   D0,$400500

3. (b)   MOVEQ   #5,D3
                 ADDQ   #1,D3

    (c)   ADD.B   (A1)+,D0
                 ADD.W   (A1),D1

    (d)   BTST   #4,D2
                 BEQ   ZERO
                 BRA   LOOP

5. (a) CODE = $100, VALUE = $107, DIGIT = $108, MAIN = $200

    (b) The contents of memory address VALUE will be $34

Chapter 6

1. (a) 16,384   (b) 11

3. On average, a read request will take
    $$t_{read} = ht_c + (1-h)t_m = 0.95 \times 20 + 0.05 \times 100 = 24 \text{ ns}$$

    As a write-through policy is used, the write time t_{write} will be the same as the main memory access time, which is 100 ns.

    Therefore the average access time of the system is given by:
    $$t_{av} = 0.85 \times t_{read} + 0.15 \times t_{write} = 0.85 \times 24 + 0.15 \times 100 = 35 \text{ ns}$$

4. The cache set will contain the blocks B, D, A, E with block counters set to 0, 1, 2 and 3 respectively.

6. (a) 203 MB   (b) 1.03 MB/second

Chapter 7

2. The PC and SR are automatically preserved because they are altered by all service routines. Because the other registers used depend upon the particular service routine, the overhead of automatically preserving them every time an interrupt takes place is not warranted. For this reason, the task of pushing these other registers onto the stack before using them and pulling them from the stack afterwards, is left to the service routine.

3. Clock cycles per second used for polling = $10 \times 50 = 500$

    Fraction of the processor clock cycles used = $\dfrac{500}{100 \times 10^6} = 0.0005\%$

Chapter 8

3. FCFS scheduling

6. A semaphore is a flag, bit or combination of bits, used to signal events. The advantage of using semaphores is that they avoid busy-waiting loops that waste the processing resource.

7.

frame 4	frame 3	frame 2	frame 1
empty	empty	empty	0 (fault)
empty	empty	0	1 (fault)
empty	0	1	2 (fault)
0	1	2	3 (fault)
1	2	3	4 (fault)
1	2	4	3
1	4	3	2
4	3	2	5 (fault)
3	2	5	6 (fault)
2	5	6	3
5	6	3	4 (fault)
6	3	4	5
3	4	5	6
4	5	6	3
4	6	3	5
6	3	5	0 (fault)

Therefore there are 9 page faults.

Chapter 9

8. (i) np_b (ii) $n(1 - p_b)$ (iii) $np_b p_t$ (iv) $np_b(1 - p_t)$

(v) $n(1 - p_b) + np_b(1 - p_t) + np_b p_t(1 + b)$

(vi) $CPI_{av} = 1 - p_b + p_b(1 - p_t) + p_b p_t(1 + b) = 1 + bp_b p_t$

9. *For first part see text*

Number of instructions per word = 256/32 = 8
Therefore 8 instructions executed per clock cycle.
Number of clock cycles per second = 100×10^6
Therefore $8 \times 100 \times 10^6 = 800$ Million Instructions per Second

Chapter 10

8. $N = 2^4 = 16$ nodes
     Path length $= \log_2 16 = 4$

     For transputer array, path length $= 2\,(\sqrt{16} - 1) = 6$

10.   Speedup $= 16\,/\,((16{-}1) \times 0.25 + 1) = 16\,/\,4.75 = 3.4$

Index

Acronyms

ACIA	Asynchronous Communication Interface Adapter
ALU	Arithmetic and Logic Unit
ASCII	American Standard Code for Information Interchange
BCD	Binary Coded Decimal
CCR	Condition Code Register
CD-R	Compact Disk-Recordable
CD-ROM	Compact Disk-Read Only Memory
CISC	Complex Instruction Set Computer
CMOS	Complementary Metal Oxide Semiconductor
CPU	Central Processing Unit
CRT	Cathode Ray Tube
CU	Control Unit
DMA	Direct Memory Access
DOS	Disk Operating System
DRAM	Dynamic Random Access Memory
EDC/ECC	Error Detection Code/Error Correction Code
EEPROM	Electrically Erasable Programmable Read Only Memory
EPROM	Erasable Programmable Read Only Memory
FCFS	First-Come-First-Served
FET	Field Effect Transistor
FIFO	First-In-First-Out
GB	Gigabyte
GUI	Graphical User Interface
HEX	Hexadecimal
HLL	High Level Language
HMOS	High Speed Metal Oxide Semiconductor
IC	Integrated Circuit
IO	Input Output
IR	Instruction Register
KB	Kilobyte
LIFO	Last-In-First-Out
LRU	Least Recently Used
LSB	Least Significant Bit
MAR	Memory Address Register
MB	Megabyte
MBR	Memory Buffer Register
MFM	Modified Frequency Modulation

MIMD	Multiple Instruction stream-Multiple Data stream
MIPS	Million Instructions Per Second
MISD	Multiple Instruction stream-Single Data stream
MMU	Memory Management Unit
MODEM	MODulator DEModulator
MOS	Metal Oxide Semiconductor
MOSFET	Metal Oxide Semiconductor Field Effect Transistor
MSB	Most Significant Bit
NMOS	N-channel Metal Oxide Semiconductor
OS	Operating System
PC	Program Counter
PCB	Printed Circuit Board
PLA	Programmed Logic Array
PMOS	P-channel Metal Oxide Semiconductor
PROM	Programmable Read Only Memory
RAM	Random Access Memory
RISC	Reduced Instruction Set Computer
RLL	Run Length Limit
ROM	Read Only Memory
RR	Round Robin
RTE	ReTurn from Exception
RTL	Register Transfer Language
RTS	ReTurn from Subroutine
R/W	Read/Write
SIMD	Single Instruction stream-Multiple Data stream
SIMM	Single In-line Memory Module
SIPO	Serial-In-Parallel-Out
SISD	Single Instruction stream-Single data stream
SP	Stack Pointer
SPARC	Scalable Processor ARChitecture
SR	Status Register
SRAM	Static Random Access Memory
TAS	Test And Set
VIA	Versatile Interface Adapter
VLIW	Very Long Instruction Word
VLSI	Very Large Scale Integration
WORM	Write-Once Read Many times
WREM	Write-Read-Erase Memory